GOD IS NOT WHO YOU THINK

GOD IS NOT WHO YOU THINK

MICHAEL GULLATTE

XULON PRESS

Xulon Press
2301 Lucien Way #415
Maitland, FL 32751
407.339.4217
www.xulonpress.com

Paperback ISBN-13: 978-1-66287-389-8

Ebook ISBN-13: 978-1-66287-390-4

TABLE OF CONTENTS

Chapter One

GOD IS NOT WHO YOU THINK

IT ALL HAPPENED in the southeastern United States in the '70s where I grew up, and nobody taught me something I did not need to know. The smells of fall had come and gone, the rose bushes refused to blossom, and the fresh, distinct smell of the first fireplace burning of the season was now the smell of smoky odor in the air. In protest, the northern waterfowl birds headed south for the dreaded winter season, which had arrived. Never judge a day by its weather.

My mother was married at nineteen and gave birth to three boys. After a few years in the marriage, her husband tragically died in a car accident. She became a widow at the age of twenty-three. Although Mom never remarried, she had a relationship with a man I would later find out was my father.

When I learned the truth, I was playing with friends and relatives in the yard at eight years old. The kids were kids by name-calling and speaking unkind things to one another. One of the kids commented on my father, and I responded firmly, "Don't you talk about my daddy. He died in a car accident!" A few of the kids, seemingly in unison, said, "Your daddy is not dead. He lives far away and doesn't want to see you," and, "Your mom was going to give you up for adoption when you were a baby." I responded with pushing and shoving until an adult broke up the fight. Later that evening, I explained the fight to Mom, and she looked at me as if to say, "I have dreaded this day."

She explained, "You are here, you are loved, and you were not given for adoption." She continued to share that my father was not dead. He made no effort to have a relationship, and she said there was never a good time to talk about this subject. She had contemplated for years over when would be the best time. It was the worst day of my childhood.

As I wept uncontrollably, I thought, "How could I be the last to know?" I felt bewildered by the thought of being born in shame and embarrassment. Mom also consoled me and cried. The playground was never the same after that day from hell. Children often said, "My mom said I can't play with you anymore because you are a bastard." I spent countless nights sobbing on my pillow and feeling no sense of self-worth. During that time, Mom made significant changes in her personal life to provide me with much-needed emotional support.

I am sure my mother called my father; months later, he stopped by for a visit. During that visit, he promised to pick me up for a long weekend of fishing and fun. A couple of months had passed, and I recall the excitement of helping Mom pack my bag for that long weekend with my father. We lived in a five-room home of 775 square feet. I shared one of the two bedrooms with my three brothers. A very used love seat overlooked the small front yard and driveway. I positioned myself on that loveseat with my little suitcase in hand, anxiously awaiting.

He did not arrive at the appointed time, so Mom insisted that he was not coming and suggested we should unpack. I was certainly not convinced, and she permitted me to stay up a little longer. After a while, I fell asleep on the loveseat and was awakened by the neighbors' chickens the following day. Sometimes it would be a month or two before I got the next call. He was very apologetic and had many excuses for why he did not show up. My friends always asked how my fishing trip went, and I would lie and tell them how much fun we had and about all the fish we caught. My father promised that we would spend weekends together throughout my childhood; truth be told, not one weekend with him ever came.

My childhood was full of broken promises from my father. After enduring years of childhood trauma, I often thought that life would have been easier if the truth about him being alive was never told.

Life goes on. My aunts, uncles, relatives, and friends worked primarily in cotton mill jobs, and there were nearly daily conversations about systemic racism. While visiting my friends' homes in the neighborhood, the conversation at their dinner table was the same. My mom would often take me along to see her friends in different communities, and the discussion eventually evolved into unfair treatment at work or in the marketplace.

Although those conversations throughout Cleveland County were well understood, our native home and beloved Shelby, North Carolina, was also home to Thomas Dixon. According to ncdcr.gov, Dixon wrote in 1901 his first novel, *The Leopard's Spots*, which called for the exclusion of blacks from American society and for reconciliation between North and South. He wrote two more books with similar messages and, in 1905, adapted one of them into a play entitled *The Clansman*. D. W. Griffith went on to adapt the play into the landmark motion picture, *The Birth of a Nation*, in 1915. According to en.wikipedia.org, the film was controversial even before its release and has remained so ever since; it has been called "the most controversial film ever made in the United States" and "the most reprehensibly racist film in Hollywood history."

Chapter Two

A CASUAL CONVERSATION WITH GOD

As a teenager, sports, drinking, and girls helped me escape my reality if only for a few hours. One wrong decision led to another, and my girlfriend was pregnant with her second child. I became a statistic. According to nyu.edu, the likelihood of graduating from college was eight percentage points less among those who lived in single-parent families than their peers with two-parent families during the '80s. The statistics showed that I had less than a ten percent chance of graduating college and becoming successful.

My mom did not earn enough at her mill job to care for a growing family of four boys. She would often take me to stand in the long welfare line for food stamps, government cheese, and other commodities. On occasions, the utilities were interrupted for non-payment. We had an old kerosene heater that provided a backup source of heat. Once again, they disconnected the utilities, and we had no money for kerosene on a brutally cold winter night; the wind was howling and blowing the gray duct-taped plastic off the broken bedroom window. We had packed up to go to Grandma's that night. I was mad at God, the brutally cold weather, my life, and my circumstances.

I told Mom that I was not going to Grandma's that night. She said, "Boy, you will freeze to death if you stay here!" I told her that it was not a bad idea so I could meet this prejudiced God, the one whose goodness Grandma was always singing about. I refused to leave and was determined to have it out with God that night. The winter months seemed twice as long and bitterly colder during those days.

And then God breathe the breath of life

It seemed that the weather dictated the community's emotions and spiritual well-being. If the day was sunny, they were happy. If the day was overcast and cold, people appeared to be depressed. Nevertheless, what happened next taught me never to let the weather dictate the kind of day I wanted to have. I positioned myself on the bottom bunk bed, crying and screaming at the top of my lungs, "God, if you are real, answer and tell me why you hate colored people and me so much!"

And then, God breathed at that moment, the glory of the Lord filling the house. The aura was breathtaking, the wind went calm, and the chill in the house fled from His presence. It suddenly felt like a springtime evening. He spoke to me audibly as a man speaks to a friend. God said, "Michael, your problem is not the color of your skin, it is your culture and your sins. Now come, let us reason together..."

The next day, I shared that conversation with my Grandma Thelma. I asked her how I could be sure He could be trusted after my childhood trauma and all the stories of racism happening to good people. She always had the right words to say, and without blinking an eye, she said, "God is faithful to those that are faithful to Him. Maybe they are not being faithful to Him. Why don't you do the right thing to prove Him wrong?" I agreed with her and immediately started making changes to prove that God had favorites and that life was sort of like the lottery system: if you lived long enough, you might occasionally get lucky and something good would happen.

Doing the right thing would include spending countless hours with God and making Him my priority, in addition to setting things right with my girlfriend, Tarsha. Although we attempted to care for two children as teenagers, we made a new commitment to God which included no physical intimacy until we were married. In addition, we committed to reading and meditating on His word to discover more about this mysterious and possibly prejudiced God.

Shortly afterward, the Lord revealed the meaning of "...your problem is your culture and your sins." I had allowed experiences that were not only my own but primarily those of my family, culture, and community to destroy my impulse to dream. Author Richard Wright in his book "black boy," said, "The impulse to dream will slowly be beating out of you through the experience of life."

A community of people was teaching me things that I did not need to know. There were overwhelming discussions about all things negative and very few conversations about personal progress and success. I had become so well-adjusted to the conversations and culture that I blended in without giving it a second thought.

Over the preceding months, the outward condition or circumstances had not changed. I was still working for a farmer tending his sheep and installing cattle fences in pastures for $25 per day, but internally a metamorphosis was happening. I was developing unconventional thinking and began to dream and have visions of a better life that would impact the community and the world.

I had thoughts of community racial reconciliation and forgiveness. A sense of self-worth, unexplainable joy and beauty transformed my mind. My thoughts were reshaping my reality. As a person thinks in their heart, so are they. And as they continue to think so, they will remain. We cannot separate who we are or whom we will become from our dominant thoughts. In his book, *As a Man, Thinketh*, author James Allen said, "Man is the master of thought, the molder of character, and the maker and shaper of condition, environment, and destiny." Those who cherish a beautiful vision, a lofty ideal in their heart, will one day realize it.

Chapter Three

THE INTERNAL GPS

THE HOLY SPIRIT became my Global Positioning System (GPS), and He positioned himself within my heart, navigating my every move and thought. That audible voice I once heard resided in my spirit. "Don't watch that...," "You're doing a good job...," "Be patient; it will happen, but not overnight...," "Let me show you something in My word..." That is how I discovered passages like Romans chapter two:

> *"But glory and honor and [heart] peace shall be awarded to everyone who [habitually] does good, the Jew first and also the Greek (Gentile). For God shows no partiality [undue favor or unfairness; with Him, one man is not different from another]."* (Romans 2:10, (Amplified Classic Version).

He was not who I once thought.

As I continued to feast on the word of God, He led me to a passage that expedited my metamorphosis. I read it as if He was speaking directly:

> *"Michael, work willingly and heartily from your soul at whatever you do, as though you were working for me rather than for people, and I will give you an inheritance as your reward."* (Colossians 3:23, New Kings James Version)

At that moment, my mind determined that I would be the best sheep keeper and cattle fence installer the farmer had ever employed. I vowed that whatever my future occupations would be, my employers would miss me when I was gone.

God said, *"Before I formed you in the womb I knew you; Before you were born I sanctified you; I ordained you a prophet to the nations."* (Jeremiah 1:5 New Kings James Version). He consecrated you; and appointed you to a particular purpose. Before time began, He declared that He knew the plans He had for you, which were plans for our well-being and never for evil, to give you an excellent and satisfying future.

A few months after we made our new commitments to the Lord, a local bank hired me as a mail courier. I entered a strange and unexplored world. In Robert Kiyosaki's book *Rich Dad Poor Dad*, he talked about the two leading influential fathers in his life. "Rich Dad" believed in financial education, learning how money works, and understanding how to put the power of money to work for him. "Poor Dad" believed in studying hard, getting good grades, and finding a well-paying job. Yet, despite his incredible attributes, "Poor Dad" didn't do well financially.

We assume that one person suffers because of their moral attributes and the other prospers because of their immoral features. If the truth is told, neither one may have excellent moral or immoral characteristics. Still, the corrupt person thrives because of their good qualities of putting the power of money to work, and the poor person lives in lack because of poor attributes of financial stewardship.

God knows what He's doing, He's got everything figured out

My new career at the bank was like having two families. One of my first family's greatest attributes was, "It is better to be poor and honest than to be dishonest and rich." I desired to be honest and prosperous to advance God's Kingdom here on earth. As I delivered mail to various offices for my second family, I often secretly listened and made notes of their discussions about real estate investments and money management. It was like a free financial management class. I was getting a good education on putting the power of money to work. What I could not learn from my first family, I gained money management knowledge from the second one.

I picked up a couple of additional part-time jobs to save money to buy a home for my new family. The Lord gave me a budget and a plan, and within months I saved enough money to make a down payment on a home. I was a homeowner at nineteen years old!

Tarsha and I were married a year later. The true knowledge of God transformed my mind. A few years after that, Tarsha was pregnant with our third child, and the internal "GPS" gave me a divine idea. We needed a home with more space, so we purchased our second home and rented out the first. The rental income was enough to pay both mortgages. God knows what He's doing. He has it all figured out.

Some of the achievements in the community of Cleveland county, NC surpassed people of any nationality, religion, or ethnicity. I worked as if the Lord was my employer and supervisor. In doing so, it was only a couple of years as a mail courier before I became the first African American in the bank's history to be promoted to the loan department.

One day, I was headed to lunch and observed the senior vice president (SVP) returning from Wednesday's "golf meeting" in his new company car. We had two old cars at home, and one of them was ready to be put out to pasture. I said to the Lord, "Why can't I have a company car?" And he said, "Michael, you have never asked me for a company car."

And I said, "Lord, I would like to have a new company car someday!"

Six months passed, and I had forgotten about the conversation, but I was reminded when that same SVP stopped by my desk and said, "Michael, I don't know of a single person in the bank that deserves this as much as you." He tossed me the keys to a brand-new Ford Crown Victoria and a bank credit card to keep it clean and fueled.

I had made a life change from working for people to working as if the Lord was my employer, which proved to have great benefits and dividends.

I worked diligently at every task over a fourteen-year banking career with two different banks. I became the first African American in the bank's history to be appointed to a commercial loan officer position and the first African American vice president of another bank. After my banking career, we founded the first multicultural church in the community and rescue missions. Those beautiful visions once cherished in our hearts had become our reality.

The new church led the community in racial reconciliation and forgiveness. There were progressive suppers taking place throughout the community. The missions served individuals throughout the United States and as far away as Russia. We received multiple visits from organizations throughout the country and the North Carolina state legislators to discover how we managed to have a greater than 75% success rate in rescue mission work. I also initiated a network of more than one hundred churches of various denominations to meet the needs of the most vulnerable individuals in our community and to come together weekly for a fellowship luncheon and prayer.

Over the years, I've received multiple awards and recognitions such as "The Spirit of Freedom" award given to a Cleveland County resident that exemplified values such as integrity, respect for individual freedom, community, self-responsibility, and lifelong learning. A foundation named me their top pick of five individuals in the entire state who were awarded for being dedicated to improving the quality of life for all North Carolinians.

When we announced our intentions of leaving our hometown to follow the Lord's leading toward ministry on The Big Island of Hawai'i, we were the only couple in the county's history that had ever been honored with an appreciation parade for years of faithful service throughout the city and county. At the appreciation luncheon, we received recognition from a senator on behalf of the state of North Carolina for making the state a better place through the hundreds of success stories from the people we served.

Using the right tools

We have traveled halfway around the globe, witnessed countless miracles, and shared the gospel in multiple countries, including church developments and well projects in West Africa, and other countries. I am a product of a single parent who dedicated her life to her family. I married at twenty years old and have been married for more than thirty years. I graduated from college "with highest honors." I superseded the statistics on education, marriage, and growing up black in America in a single-parent home.

And, If I can do it, I believe anyone can and will become successful with the right tools. It was a fact that communities in the South have endured nearly a lifetime of systemic racism. But the truth is, it does not matter about your ethnicity, dilemma, or current circumstances; we have what it takes to rise above the opposition and whatever systems are in place to hinder us from moving forward if we work His plan (Ephesians 6:10-18). I wrote this book to provide God-given insight and revelation for domination by following practical principles in every area of your life.

Chapter Four

THE CHATTER IS
WHAT MATTERS

WE BECOME INCAPABLE of functioning or surviving if our thoughts become unstable. Destabilized thoughts will have a direct impact on our language and culture. And that is why we should stand out and not fit in with our culture as it was with the three young Jewish men who became enslaved people under the power of the evil King Nebuchadnezzar II. (Daniel 3) The evil king attempted to destabilize their thoughts and language by teaching them the Babylonian system and culture and giving them Babylonian names.

The king decreed that everyone who heard the sound of the horn, flute, harp, lyre, and psaltery, in harmony with all kinds of music, was required to fall and worship the golden image. Those who disobeyed were to be thrown into the fiery furnace. The king was told that three young Jewish men were disrespecting his ordinance, refusing to serve the king's gods or worship the image. They replied to the king that it was true and did not need to answer him on the matter. The three exclaimed that the God they served was able to deliver them from the furnace and, for whatever reason, He chose not to deliver them; they would not worship his golden image. Their response infuriated the king, but those men held to what they believed and were rescued. They stayed true to their cause, and I think they were able to do it with good self-talk as one of their core character traits.

You would have to search long and hard to find someone that has held more critical offices in the history of the United States than John Quincy Adams.

He served with distinction as president, senator, congressman, and minister to major European powers. He participated in various capacities in the American Revolution, the War of 1812, and events leading to the Civil War.

Yet, at the age of 70, with much of that behind him, he sadly said, "My whole life has been a succession of disappointments, and I can scarcely recollect a single instance of success in anything that I ever undertook." Adams decreed that life had been a succession of disappointments, perhaps he entertained the internal negative chatter. (Source: Sermon Illustrations Charles Sell, Unfinished Business, Multnomah, 1989, p. 233.)

Create what will be through intentional thinking

The food of thought will either satisfy or cause depression, yield a harvest or bondage. Our evil thoughts will bring forth bad results, while great wholesome thoughts produce after their kind and bring along great results.

We should rather speak words of wisdom as Paul did in 2 Corinthians 4:8 (NKJV); he said that although he was pressed on every side by troubles, he was not crushed. He was perplexed but not driven to despair. Perhaps persecuted but never abandoned by God. He decreed that his present problems were minor (merely light afflictions) that would not last very long. God has wholesome thoughts about you.

He said to Jeremiah, I know the thoughts that I think toward you, thoughts of peace, and not of evil, to give you an expected end." (Jeremiah 29:11 NKJV) His thoughts toward you are much higher and vast than the mind can imagine. *The Message* Bible, Jeremiah 29:11 says, "I'll show up and take care of you as I promised and bring you back home. I know what I'm doing. I have it all planned out—plans to take care of you, not abandon you, plans to give you the future you hope for."

The idiom "seeing is believing" is in direct contrast to how we should think. The renewed mind thinks, "If I can believe it, I will see it manifest in my life." According to en.wikipedia.org, "que sera, sera" (whatever will be, will be) was introduced by a Doris Day song in the 1956 Alfred Hitchcock film *The Man Who Knew Too Much*. The song received an Academy Award and other recognitions, and our culture still sings it to this day, but a mind that has been transformed understands that it could not be further from the truth, that whatever will be will be. We have been given the power and authority to create what "will be" through intentional thinking. Destiny is determined by everyone knowing who they are in Christ Jesus and not what someone told them.

Your words are like thought seeds and will and shall produce after their kind. Negative situations and circumstances are birthed out of the germination of negative thoughts. We cannot separate who we are, how we live, or what we will become from our most dominant thoughts. Nothing comes from tomato seeds but tomatoes, and nothing comes from avocado seeds but avocados. Nothing comes from negative thoughts but unfavorable circumstances and situations, and nothing comes from positive thoughts but daily favor and blessings (Psalm 68:19).

It's impossible to keep your thoughts quiet or secret; they will eventually form good or bad habits and be on full display for everyone to see. Out of the plethora of thoughts, the mouth speaks. Your words have the power to put an end to fiery circumstances, cut the head off a gigantic situation, or set a forest on fire. Choose wisely.

Equipped with a small powerful weapon

It is comforting to know that before the Earth's foundations, before God drew up blueprints and measurements of the Earth, before He commanded the light to appear and gave darkness a home, and even before the heavens had ordinances of their rule, God had a plan for your life. As often as I can remind you, I want you to know that His plan is still good with no expiration date! His gifts and callings on your life are without repentance. Perhaps you have gone through multiple divorces, had an abortion, or lived a life of crime. He has not changed His mind because you made some mistakes along the way. There is nothing you have done or will do that catches Him by surprise. He knew it before you did it. The gifts and callings are still there and waiting on you to receive!

The cross's message is only foolish to those who head toward destruction. But those that are saved know it is the very power of God, the same power that raised Jesus from the dead, living on the inside of us! Hallelujah!

> *Yes, I know it sounds a little foolish to the ears, but I want you to know that this ridiculous plan of God is wiser than the wisest of human plans, and God's weakness is stronger than the greatest of human strength. Let me tell you another way; God chose things the world considers foolish to shame those who think they are wise. And he chose things that are powerless to shame those who are powerful. He chose things despised by the world, those counted as nothing, and used them to bring to nothing that the world considers necessary.* (1 Corinthians 1:18 Msg. Bible).

Although we have our being in the flesh, we don't fight as the military does by using physical weapons. God has equipped us with spiritual weapons like our tongue, which is a mighty weapon. The symphony of the sea weighs more than two hundred and twenty-five thousand tons but is controlled by a small rudder, and the tongue, as small as it is, controls the entire body. The king of the jungle silently sleeps in the belly of the lioness. The embryo of the mighty fifty foot and 75,000-pound whale shark pup patiently waits within its mother's egg. The remarkable two-hundred-and-seventy-five-foot General Sherman tree lives in the seed. Our dreams, desires, and destiny wait patiently in the confinements of our minds. The mind is the great manufacturer of anything it receives.

Gifts with no expiration date

Our little tongue will cause our thoughts to germinate. It will pullulate like the embryo of the whale shark and seeds in a garden to bring forth words of destruction or liberation. You get to choose. I want to share invisible weapons lying dormant within you, awaiting an opportunity to bring transformation, prosperity, and joy amid trouble beyond understanding. They are like undiscovered gifts that has not expired.

Chapter Five

ARMED AND DANGEROUS –
LIVING IN THE BUBBLE

*The gladiators fought a battle using weapons of metal and steel,
but we wrestle not against people but spiritual wickedness. We
war against spirits; to fight a spirit, we must war in the Spirit.*
(Ephesians 6:10-18 NKJV).

THE PROPHET ZECHARIAH prophesied that Jerusalem would one
day be so full of people and livestock that there would not be room enough
for everyone, and he said that many would live outside the protection of
the city walls.

*Then, the Lord Himself will be a protective firewall around
Jerusalem, and He will be the glory inside the city.* (Zechariah
2:4-5 NLT)

Zechariah prophesied that the Lord would protect them with His invisible
shield. The people would live somewhat of a "spiritual bubble," and to guar-
antee our success, the Lord has given us His invisible shields, a.k.a. "spiritual
bubble." The weapons of our warfare are not worldly or earthly but mighty
in God for the pulling down of strongholds. Paul appealed to us, *"Put on
the whole armor of God."* The armor is the same invisible shield that Satan
recognized God had given to Job. Satan presented himself with the angels;
he told God that Job was hedged-in (fortified) so tight that he couldn't get
to him (Job 1:9-10 NKJV).

However, Job often proclaimed that his children had sinned, and he habitually made sacrifices on their behalf (Job 1:5 NKJV). When catastrophe came to Job, he said, "For the thing, I greatly feared has come upon me, and what I dreaded has happened to me." (Job 3:24-25 NKJV). Could it be that Job's greatest fears concerned his children and material possessions?

It is said more than fifty times in the scriptures, "Do not fear, don't be afraid." When we begin to worry and become frightened, the enemy chips away at our invisible shield like a sledgehammer chipping away at a concrete block. Once our shield is penetrated, just like a hairline fracture in concrete, it becomes exposed and susceptible to further damage. Seeds of doubt, worry, and unbelief are given a passageway to enter.

The mind is the battlefield

It is of the utmost importance that we keep our heads on straight. We expect to win every battle and overcome every affliction (Psalm 34:19 New King James Version). The helmet of salvation enables us to be transformed by the entire renewal of our mind by its new ideas and a new attitude. Whether we think positively or negatively, our minds begin to manufacture those released words in the atmosphere.

Those negative thoughts are like weeds; they spread rapidly and suffocate positive growth. Weeds produce after their kind, and if they go unchecked for some time, they will consume the garden and its vines. Like negative thoughts, weeds don't need much nurturing to grow. They sprout under any condition. Like weeds, thoughts must be cultivated consistently.

Jesus said, "Therefore, take no thought, saying...." (Matthew 6:31 KJV)

The evidence that we have taken a thought is followed by what we say. So, we take the negative thoughts captive to protect our invisible shield. In John 13:2, the devil had already "put the thought" in Judas to betray Jesus.

Judas could have chosen to bring that thought under subjection or become enslaved to it, and he chose the latter. Judas's story reminds us to refute reasonings and ideologies in our minds that are contrary to the word of God. And we take all the armor that the word of God instructs us to take. He's given it to us so that we may stand up against every trick and scheme of the evil one. Our changing world doesn't change us.

> *The Lord wishes above all things that we prosper and*
> *be in health, even as our soul prospers and keeps well.*
> (3 John 1:2 NKJV)

The invisible weapon, the "helmet of salvation," is also about redemption and preservation. Webster's *American Dictionary of the English Language* of 1828 defines salvation as the deliverance from our eternal death.

"Freedom does not mean I am able to do whatever I want to do. That's the worst kind of bondage. Freedom means I have been set free to become all that God wants me to be, to achieve all that God wants me to achieve, to enjoy all that God wants me to enjoy." Warren Wiersbe.

When we understand why we've been preserved, we become eager students to learn, and the world becomes our library.

Salvation means to be saved, rescued, and delivered. (Source: Precept Austin Greek Word Study) In Exodus 14, the children of Israel had no sooner left Egypt during the Passover night to find themselves surrounded by mountains, the sea in front of them, and a very angry Pharaoh and his mighty army pressing in from the rear. The people panicked and blamed Moses for leading them to the wilderness to die. The people exclaimed that it was better to die as enslaved people in Egypt than as a corpse in the wilderness. But Moses told the people to be confident and see the salvation of the Lord, which He would show them on that very day. And they were miraculously rescued and preserved that day.

When we take the helmet of salvation, we take the invisible shield or the spiritual bubble. *Preservation* is to maintain something in its actual existence. (Webster, 1828) Jesus's finished work on the cross, a.k.a. "atonement," guaranteed our protection in this life and the eternal life to come. It doesn't mean that negative things will not happen, but you are guaranteed to overcome every one of them. (1 Corinthians 10:12)

In 1795, Napoleon Bonaparte offered a reward for whoever could develop a safe, reliable food preservation method for his constantly traveling army. About fifteen years later, Nicholas Appert took on the challenge and introduced a technique that involved heat-processing food in glass jars reinforced with wire and sealing them with wax. (Source: www.thespruceeats.com)

The preservation method conserved fruits and vegetables that were freshly picked. My late Grandma Thelma perfected the modern-day canning process where she sealed the jars and, two years later, she opened the canned fruits and vegetables, which tasted like they were freshly picked from the vine.

Chapter Six

KEEPING THE LITTLE FOX FROM SPOILING THE VINE

SALVATION IS ABOUT preserving our conscience and restoring us to our original intent. Our sins become justified [Just-If-I'd] never sinned, as Paul explained to the men of Israel while preaching in the synagogue at Antioch in Pisidia.

> *"Therefore, let it be known to you, brethren, that through this Man is preached to you the forgiveness of sins; 39 and by Him, everyone who believes is justified from all things from which you could not be justified by the law of Moses."* (Acts 13:38-39 NKJV)

Justified, just-if-I'd never sinned

We are what we think in our hearts. (Proverbs 23:7) The renewed mind thinks, "I am just-if-I'd..." never sinned. However, when evil comes our way, the renewed thinking will immediately know this trouble did not come from God. If anything negative happens in our family, Tarsha and I will immediately say in the Southern way of talking, "That's not God!"

Whether the fires that come are natural or manufactured, they did not come from the Lord because He doesn't send trouble to destroy his people. Now that we have more knowledge of the Helmet of Salvation, Paul explains in 2 Corinthians 5:16-21 (NLT) the responsibilities of a good soldier:

> «*So, we have stopped evaluating others from a human point of view. At one time, we thought of Christ merely from a human point of view. How differently we know him now!* [17] *This means that anyone who belongs to Christ has become a new person. The old life is gone; a new life has begun!* [18] *And all of this is a gift from God, who brought us back to himself through Christ. And God has given us this task of reconciling people to him.* [19] *For God was in Christ, reconciling the world to himself, no longer counting people's sins against them. And he gave us this wonderful message of reconciliation.* [20] *So we are Christ's ambassadors; God makes his appeal through us. We speak for Christ when we plead, "Come back to God!"* [21] *For God made Christ, who never sinned, to be the offering for our sin so that we could be made right with God through Christ."*
> (2 Corinthians 5:16-21 New Living Translation).

God is not in the sin business, nor in the business of tempting His children to sin.

> "*Blessed is a man who perseveres under trial; for once he has been approved, he will receive the crown of life which the Lord has promised to those who love Him.* [13] *No one is to say when he is tempted, "God is tempting me"; for God cannot be tempted by evil, and He does not tempt anyone."* (James 1:12-18 New American Standard Bible)

Many individuals interpret God's will by their circumstances and are confused when they are bombarded with many cases. We analyze the will of God for our lives through the scriptures. And God cannot change His mind about what He's already said, "*My covenant I will not break, nor alter the word that has gone out of My lips. (Psalm 89:34 NKJV).* Because healthy eaters think healthy, they are attracted to healthy restaurants, healthy food stores, and other healthy-eating people. Like healthy eaters, if you control your thoughts, a positive change in your life is soon to come. May you continue to remind yourself that God doesn't send evil to terrorize His people and did not send His Son to cause us to fear.

According to John 10:10 (NASB), Jesus said, *"The thief comes only to steal and kill and destroy; I came so that they would have life and have it abundantly."*

In the '70s when I was in elementary school, if a student asked to go to the bathroom during class and permission was granted, the teacher would give the student a massive wooden pass inscribed with the teacher's name and classroom number.

The big wooden pass notified every principal, faculty, and staff member in the hallway that Mrs. Duncan permitted me to go. Likewise, if God allowed or helped cause a crisis or tragedy, it means that He signed off on it and granted permission to the thief to kill, steal, or destroy us.

Suppose you received a call from someone you dearly love and they are hysterically screaming at you, "How could you allow this to happen! Why did you not prevent it?" Your loved one's car has broken down on the freeway overpass during rush hour traffic, and they blame you.

Although you are very disappointed that they would even think you had something to do with their situation, you give your best effort to convince them otherwise. Emotions have gotten the best of them, so they are not convinced you didn't have something to do with this adverse event, but they ask you to come immediately to the rescue.

Upon your arrival, they jump out of the car in unbelievable excitement and exclaim, "I can't believe you came, but I am so excited that you did!" How would you feel at that moment? Perhaps you would feel confused, disappointed, devastated, or betrayed.

They first accuse you of causing their misfortune as they ask you to help, and then they are surprised that you showed up. In my opinion, I believe many people have this roller-coaster relationship with God. Although we know how to give good gifts to those we love, how much more will our heavenly Father give good gifts to those who ask Him? (Matthew 7:11)

The CDC reports that more than two million people are injured yearly from motor vehicle accidents, and I believe God is blamed for most of them or aiding and abetting. I can only imagine the Lord explaining to the victims that He would never do such a thing, "the thief comes not but to kill, steal and destroy. But I have come that you might have life and have it more abundantly." (John 10:10) The Lord's best efforts failed to convince them that He was not to blame.

Solomon exclaimed in Proverbs 18:20-21 (NLT) *"Wise words satisfy like a good meal; the right words bring satisfaction. The tongue can bring death or life; those who love to talk will reap the consequences."* In the Song of Solomon 2:15 NKJV, he also said, *"Catch us the foxes, the little foxes that spoil the vines, for our vines have tender grapes."* The little foxes were chewing the vines and preventing the possibility of a harvest. Procrastination, narrow mindedness, and the lack of knowledge are like the foxes that spoils the vine, especially when we misunderstand the power of misplaced words. When we have confidence, it is that assurance of our minds and belief in the integrity of the creator.

Chapter Seven

THE SMALL SUSTAINER
OF LIFE

WE SOMETIMES FIND ourselves in situations where we can't see a way out. During those times, you might ask yourself, "How will I ever be able to get out of this jam?" Fighting an excellent spiritual battle includes believing the invisible "how." Although you can't see your "how," it does not mean that it doesn't exist.

> *13 The temptations in your life are no different from what others experience. And God is faithful. He will not allow the temptation to be more than you can stand. When you are tempted, he will show you a way out so that you can endure.* (1 Corinthians 10:13 NLT)

As a teenager, the odds were stacked against me. Statistics had written its documentary that my life would be one of drug abuse, crime, and a familiar face in the judicial system, and there was no evidence to dispute the data of my fate. How to overcome my circumstances had not entered my mind, and I was blind to anything beyond my current reality.

> The apostle John said, *"This is the confidence that we have in Him, that if we ask anything according to His will, He hears us. And if we know that He hears us, whatever we ask, we know that we have the petitions that we have asked of Him."* (1 John 5:14 NKJV)

You are in a great position if you don't have much confidence to accomplish your task or overcome a situation that seems impossible. My confidence was depleted through the issues of life, but personal confidence was not a requirement. I needed to rely on Him to do what he promised.

So, I found his will and promises and asked accordingly. Our confidence is better served by believing that He is well able to perform what He promised, and personal belief is soon to follow. When hope against hope was gone, I learned to trust and rely on God, not myself.

The invisible "How" will soon become reality

Faith taught me to trust in what I could not naturally see or comprehend; by doing so, that invisible "how" became my reality. In Acts 27, the story is told of Paul as a prisoner on a ship on the way to Rome, finding himself amid a tremendous and violent storm where there was no daylight for several days! The storm was so bad that all on board had given up hope. And about that time, Paul stood and said, "Listen up! Last night, an angel appeared to me and said, 'Paul, don't be afraid! You must appear before Caesar, and there will be no loss of life for anyone sailing with you!' Paul told the men, "And I believe it will be exactly as the Angel said to me!" It is imperative that we believe it will be exactly like the word of God said it will be for yourself and your family.

As you fight the good fight of faith, God will preserve you from the power of evil that threatens to overtake you despite the magnitude of the hard times, afflictions, and trouble.

"The righteous cry out, and the Lord hears and rescues them from all their troubles. [18] The Lord is near the brokenhearted and saves those who are crushed in spirit. [19] The afflictions of

the righteous are many, but the Lord rescues him from them all." (Psalm 37:19 NASB)

"The Lord shall preserve you from all evil; He shall preserve your soul. ⁸ The Lord shall preserve your going out and your coming in from this time forth, and forevermore. Psalm 121:7-8 (NKJV)

What an excellent benefit package we have! And we have a fail-proof plan to multiply self-confidence when we understand the parable of the seed (Matthew 13:3). The parable was so important that Jesus said if you can't understand this one, you will not be able to understand any of them (Mark 4:13). Everything that has ever existed is a product of seed. It is the seed that sustains life. The allegory compares four types of people and how they receive and protect the word when it's sown in their hearts, as the farmer sows and protects his seed.

Solomon said, "Let not mercy and truth forsake you; Bind them around your neck, write them on the tablet of your heart, and so find favor and high esteem in the sight of God and man" (Proverbs 3:3 NKJV). How do you write on the tablet of your heart? Psalm 45 New Kings James Version gives instructions on how to write things in your heart, *"My heart is overflowing with a good theme; I recite my composition concerning the King; My tongue is the pen of a ready writer."*

We use our tongue as a pen to write things on the tablet of our hearts. Our words are like seeds; they only produce after their kind once planted.

In Proverbs 21:23 NKJV, Solomon said, *"Whoever guards his mouth and tongue keeps his soul from troubles."* I did not understand this concept as a teenager but was compelled to verbalize specific scriptures daily. By doing so, I worked as a farmer, sowing word seeds into the good soil of my heart, and what was sown caught a root and grew.

Now that we know how to write words on our hearts, we can understand the allegories of the four seeds. You are the sower, and the sower sows the word. We can interpret the Bible as a seed book that is no different from a pack of vegetable seeds. If each remains contained, they have no power or authority to produce. The Bible is like vegetable seeds and must be opened and planted to be productive. Many people will say they have a Bible App or keep the Bible in their car, but nothing becomes of a bible in the back seat of a vehicle or a pack of seeds in a drawer if they are not fulfilling their purpose to be sown.

When I was a teenager, I watched vampire and werewolf movies, and as the films displayed, I assumed a person could hold up a cross or the Bible and the evil spirits and vampires would flee. Holding up a cross and a bible no more protected me from evil spirits than standing in a garage made me a car. Placing things around doors and windows, burning sage, and eating turmeric will not protect you from evil spirits, no more than expecting a harvest by holding up an unopened pack of seeds and praying for it to produce. I found the solution to protection and growth was for me to open the book and sow the word by writing it on the tablet of my heart.

Preventing conception

In the parable of the four different seed types, it is noted that Satan took only the first seed away because of confusion and misunderstanding.

> *When anyone hears the word of the kingdom and does not understand it, then the wicked one comes and snatches away what was sown in his heart. This is he who received seed by the wayside.* (Matthew 13:29 NKJV)

That is why Solomon exclaimed that wisdom is the principal thing; in all our getting, we should get understanding. (Proverbs 4:7) The second and third seeds were voluntarily handed over to Satan because the people became offended and resentful, and the cares, anxieties, and passionate desires for other things suffocated the word.

> *20 But he who received the seed on stony places, this is he who hears the word and immediately receives it with joy; 21 yet he has no root in himself but endures only for a while. When tribulation or persecution arises because of the word, he immediately stumbles. 22 Now he who received seed among the thorns is he who hears the word, and the cares of this world and the deceitfulness of riches choke the word, and he becomes unfruitful.* (Matthew 13:20-22 NKJV)

Notice that trouble came "because" of the Word. He is not necessarily after the believer, but the seed that the believer is carrying is what he desires. Satan is only interested in whether the word will conceive inside of you, and he can't control the conception process so he uses deception, offense, and misplaced values as weapons to cause the word to be aborted.

Many evangelicals use the terminology, "New level, new devil." After receiving a new revelation, I vowed never to repeat the false phrase. There are no new devils or spirits. He's the same as he was more than five thousand years ago when he deceived Eve in the garden and persuaded her to believe something false was the truth. God said if you eat the fruit on the tree in the middle of the garden, you will die. Satan said you wouldn't die but gain more knowledge and be like God. And Eve sowed the words of Satan in her heart and became convinced that the tree was beautiful and its fruit delicious as she desired the so-called wisdom it would give her.

It was a classic game of deception. He caused Eve to desire something that she already had. She wanted to be like God, but she was already like God, without sin, and created in His image from the rib of Adam. Nevertheless, Adam was with Eve as she ate from the tree, giving him some of the fruit, and he ate. Afterward, they both felt shame at their nakedness and sewed fig leaves to cover themselves. When they heard God walking in the garden, although fig leaves covered them, they felt naked and hid.

Where was Satan, the serpent? After his deception catches root and brings rotten fruit within us, he moves on to another victim. Like us, Adam and Eve dealt with the results. Adam started the blame game when asked why he ate the forbidden tree.

Interestingly, Adam first blamed God. "The woman 'you gave me' enticed me to eat, and I ate." (Genesis 3:12) Eve blamed God and Satan. "The serpent; the serpent you created cheated and outwitted me, and I ate." (Genesis 3:13) The reality is that there is nobody to blame but us when we have more confidence in any created thing above our creator.

Adam did not give the Word Seed from God enough time to grow and mature in his heart. God granted Adam permission to eat from any tree in the garden except the Tree-of-Knowledge-of-Good-and-Evil. He said you don't eat from it; you're dead the moment you do. (Genesis 2:16)

A change of heart

How do I know if the Word of God has taken root in my heart? Does it change my behavior? Anything that changes my behavior, I have entirely understood. Whether by accident or not, touching a boiling pot with your hands should change your behavior. A behavior change confirms that you are sure to use an oven mitt glove the next time. It became apparent that Adam was not entirely convinced he would die if he ate the forbidden fruit. He had no behavior change despite the Word of God. Eve ate and offered him some fruit to eat, and he ate. A convinced heart would have forbidden Eve to touch the fruit. What should have been the shortest and simplest game of charades— *"Eve, God said we can't eat of it."* Instead, their disobedience gave birth to spiritual darkness that still covers the earth today.

The second seed in the parable fell on "rocky soil." Rocky soil is a heart that is very skeptical about whether God's Word is wholly accurate. (Matthew 13:5-6) Rocks in a garden are the same as an overwhelming amount of doubt and unbelief in the heart; both will hinder seeds from sinking deep and catching good roots. Then, when the seeds spring up, they have not enough roots, and the sun rises and scorches the seed. It withers and dies, or tribulation, affliction, and persecution come because of the word they stumble and fall away. Satan did not take away the Word Seed that said, "If you eat of the tree in the middle of the garden, you will die." The moment Adam and Eve ate the fruit, they voluntarily handed over that seed to him and deprived it of an opportunity to catch root, grow, and produce fruit.

The third seed in the parable is the people who hear the word, but the world's cares, glamour, and the deceitfulness of missing out on worldly "stuff" suffocate the word, producing no fruit. According to en.wikipedia.org, a fishing lure is a broad type of artificial fishing bait used in angling that are designed to mimic prey animals and attract the attention of predatory fish, using appearances, movements, vibrations, bright reflections, and flashy colors to appeal to the fish's predation instinct and entice it into striking. Such as Satan, our adversary, he's appealing to the lustful desires of a person's heart that longs to look influential, famous, and wealthy. A fickle mind will always be in a vulnerable state and subject to being enticed and led astray.

Matthew 13:22 AMPC says, "...delight and glamour and deceitfulness of riches choke and suffocates the Word, and it yields no fruit." It is no different from a farmer who takes much time to plant his garden, and when done, he gathers his pruned weeds and stacks them on top of the freshly sown garden; the weeds suffocate the seed.

The fourth seed is the seed that was received into the good ground or "good soil." It is noted that this seed produced a harvest of thirty, sixty, and even a hundred times as much as had been planted. Have you ever wondered why this seed was highly productive, yet the other three seeds did not produce as much as a tiny fruit, although the seeds were scattered from the same pack? To understand this mystery, we must comprehend the condition of the soil of the first three seeds. The soil (heart) of the first three seeds contained confusion, misunderstanding, skepticism, glamour, care for the world, and an overwhelming amount of doubt and unbelief. The seed is never the issue; it's all about the condition of the soil (heart).

Chapter Eight

The Best Things in Life Take Time

IN THE EARLY '90s, I purchased a real estate course on a VHS tape with a workbook. I was determined to buy an investment property with no money down, as the course proclaimed. There were countless opinions about the training system, from "It's a scam, there's not enough information to be successful" to those who expressed gratitude for the system after purchasing real estate with no money. The tape contained an audience full of those who were to receive the same seeds of wisdom, but the condition of their hearts would determine the size of their crops.

I observed those listening intently, sitting on the edge of their seats, those reclined in their chairs with arms folded, and those with bobbing heads desperately awaiting break time. A few others were listening intently, pondering what the presenter was saying, and taking notes. I decided to be like the few in the audience that listened, considered, and took notes. After several unsuccessful attempts to put my new real estate knowledge to work, we purchased our first investment property with no money. My return on investment depended on the condition of my willing heart to receive the presenter's instructions. That success did not happen by chance or luck but by sowing seeds of education from the presenter and receiving a hundred-fold return.

It is no different from the parable of the sower. The heart of the first three seeds had too much competition for space and rich nutrients. The weeds of misunderstanding, confusion, skepticism, bitterness, doubt, and unbelief are well adapted to the areas of our hearts where they are attempting to grow. They fight against the Word of God for space, nutrients, and water. When those weeds are ignored and allowed to linger in our hearts for years, they grow a deep downward and outward root system. They usually win, being the stronger competitors at this stage; if there's no severe cultivation, God's Word doesn't stand a chance.

It is fascinating how weeds in nature can germinate under harsh conditions. (Source: thespruce.com) Allelopathy comes from the Greek words *allelon* (one another or mutual) and *pathy* (suffering). It refers to a plant releasing chemicals that have some effect on another plant. Allelopathy is a survival mechanism that allows certain plants to compete and often destroy nearby plants by inhibiting seed sprouting, root development, or nutrient uptake. Allelopathic plants are those that create zones of infertility around their roots. In the parable, we could say that the three types of people were victims of allelopathy. Roots of bitterness, skepticism, misunderstanding, doubt, and unbelief created zones of infertility around their heart and inhibited seed sprouting of the Word of God.

A heart lacking in seed sprouting of the word is a life that is void of the Invisible Armor of God. The Greek meaning of allelopathy is to "cause another to suffer." Out of the abundance of the heart, the mouth speaks. A heart full of bitterness, skepticism, hatred, and misunderstanding causes others to suffer. I have known two ladies in their 90s, Rena McGinnis and Essie McSwain; their faces radiated with expressions of love and joy from hearts free of bitterness and doubt, and they appeared to be twenty years younger.

And I have also known a man in his 50s with a face marred by time and a heart full of rebellion and selfishness that caused him to appear to be in his 80s. His toxic thoughts and words caused a lasting impact on his children and others connected to him. My three friends received the product from the conditions of their hearts. The fourth seed produced thirty, sixty, and one hundred times as much as sown. Its production resulted from less "allelopathy" in the heart. It was referred to as the "good soil" because it was the heart that had fewer roots of bitterness, skepticism, misunderstanding, doubt, hatred, and unbelief. And that is the heart that will produce after its kind. Could it be that the heart that had very little "allelopathy" is the heart that produced a one-hundred-fold return?

When prayers go unanswered, we are often given a checklist from the "experts" to ensure we've dotted the i's and crossed the t's.

That list typically includes a need to pray more, binding the evil hindering spirits, lack of persistency, walking around our home seven times, buying anointing oil, and a list of other things we're either not doing or not doing good enough. My grandparents were farmers, and once they planted their seed in the well-cultivated soil, they did not have a consultation with the experts for advice on the next step.

The good soil

Although it takes time, they understood that seeds in good soil produce by themselves. It's impossible to plant the Word of God in a fertile heart and not bring forth answers to prayers and turn mountains into molehills. My grandparents never attempted to dig up their planted seeds to make sure they were in the soil, even when it seemed like germination was delayed. They had confidence that their seeds would produce after their kind in time.

C. S. Lewis once said, "You never know how much you believe anything until its truth or falsehood becomes a matter of life and death. It is easy to say you believe a rope is strong if you merely use it to wrap a box. But suppose you had to hang by that rope over a cliff. Wouldn't you then first discover how much you trusted it?" *sermonillustrations.com belief*

Do less, not more

In Mark 4:28, Jesus said the earth produces the crops on its own. "First, a leaf blade pushes through, then the heads of wheat are formed, and the grain ripens. As soon as the grain is ready, the farmer comes and harvests it with a sickle, for the harvest time has come." The parable of the sower is about doing less of a to-do list, not doing more. No "heart soil" is perfect. Still, the heart with less "allelopathy" will produce it alone. How does a person get rid of the "allelopathy?" In the old covenant, the people would fast to cause their voices to be heard on high. (Isaiah 58:4) After the death and resurrection, fasting became a tool to bring the mind of the flesh under subjection and eliminate unbelief.

Matthew 17:19 is the story of a great crowd of people awaiting Jesus at the bottom of a mountain. As he approached, a certain man stepped out of the crowd and fell at Jesus' feet, begging him to have mercy on his son. He exclaimed that his son suffers terribly from blackouts and seizures and frequently throws himself into fires and rivers. He had brought his son to the disciples, but they could not make a difference in his health. After speaking, Jesus seemed perturbed; he turned to the crowd and exclaimed that they were a faithless and unbelieving generation. Afterward, they brought the boy to Jesus, and he reprimanded the evil spirit within him, and it came out; the boy was healed from that moment. Later that day, His disciples came to him privately and asked why they could not cast it out.

> [20] So Jesus said to them, "Because of your unbelief; for assuredly, I say to you, if you have faith as a mustard seed, you will say to this mountain, 'Move from here to there,' and it will move; and nothing will be impossible for you. [21] However, this kind does not go out except by prayer and fasting." (Matthew 17:20-21 NKJV)

A solution to the unbelief problem

Jesus explained to his disciples that the evil spirit was not the issue, but their "allelopathy" of unbelief. And he continued with the solution to the unbelief problem. He said that kind of unbelief requires prayer and fasting. According to John 15:7-8 NLT, every time you sow, it is the Lord's desire for you to produce a hundred times as much as sown, and He gets excited when you do!

> *"But if you remain in me and my words remain in you, you may ask for anything you want, and it will be granted! When you produce much fruit, you are my true disciples. Producing fruit brings great glory to my Father!"* (John 15:7-8 NLT)

While the earth remains, there will be seedtime and then harvest. Seedtime does not happen overnight. Farmers will not plant today and expect a complete harvest tomorrow. They understand that seeds sown today will fulfill a future need.

Springtime sowing provides a summer harvest. Farmers plant before they need a crop, and we understand this concept in the natural world. Still, spiritually we often wait until a crisis: the physician gives us an unfavorable diagnosis, or the mortgage company sends us a certified foreclosure letter. We attempt to germinate the Word of God overnight for a breakthrough. We start the social media crisis prayer chain and find ourselves in a desperate situation. I have discovered that the best time to sow is before I have a need.

Seedtime takes time and can't be cheated. Jesus said,

> *"The Kingdom of heaven is like a man that scatterers seed on the ground, and he continues to sleep and rise night and day while the seed sprouts and grows and increases, yet he knows not how."* (Mark 4:26 NKJV).

Jesus strategically compared the Kingdom to the process of a seed because there are no shortcuts from germination time to the harvest. If He had compared it to taking an exam, there would be ways to cheat the process. As a teenager, I stayed up on more than one occasion half the night memorizing answers for a test and did exceptionally well the next day. Still, if you had asked me about the test weeks later, I could not have told you much because the answers were not rooted in my heart. He did not compare it to filing taxes because there are so many illegal and legal loopholes to save money on paying federal and state taxes. But, there are no alternatives to seed germination; the seed process cannot be manipulated. It would be safe to say that many of us have waited to the very last minute to germinate a word seed and are at a loss of what to do. I have been in such a situation, and I would like to share how I responded.

Chapter Nine

Get in Rhythm

NOW THAT WE have our heads on straight, we are ready to put on two pieces of invisible armor that go together. The Sword of the Spirit (God's Word) overpowers and crushes every plot and plan of the evil one. Paul told the saints in Ephesus to take the sword of the Spirit, which is the Word of God. (Ephesians 6:17 NKJV) The Shield of Faith and the Sword of the Spirit are inseparable.

Medieval swords were designed to be used for blows directly against the opponent's body or shield and in the edge-to-edge style of sword fighting. (Source: medieval-swords.htm) The Word of God is sharper than a surgeon's scalpel. The word not only convicts and lets us know whether we are doing things appropriately, but it also makes it possible for us to discern the intentions of others. When we became born again, we confessed that Jesus was Lord. He walked the earth as a man; he was crucified and resurrected. Salvation came by faith (believing and confessing the story of the atonement).

"By faith, we understand that the worlds were framed by the Word of God so that the things which are seen were not made of things which are visible." (Hebrews 11:3 NKJV)

God spoke the world into existence and commanded us to be imitators of Him. (Ephesians 5:1) We are to use this Sword of the Spirit, which is the Word of God, to reshape and recreate our world. The Webster 1828 dictionary defines imitate as, "to follow in manners; to copy in form; to attempt or endeavor to copy or resemble."

The *Cambridge English Dictionary* defines imitation as, "to behave in a similar way to someone or to copy their speech and behavior.

The word declares that the Lord knows the end of a thing from its beginning. He knows how the fight will turn out before it gets started. If we get in rhythm with the Lord's behavior by speaking things that do not exist as they did, we are guaranteed victory! Yet in all the troubles and afflictions that come our way, we are more than conquerors and gain surpassing success through Him Who loves us! Praise God!

He has put His Words in your mouth

The prophet Jeremiah saw himself as inadequate and only a youth when called to great work, but the Lord put His words in Jeremiah's mouth and gave him authority over nations and kingdoms—to root up, pull down, destroy, overturn, and build and plant. (Jeremiah 1:8) The story reminds me of our power as believers to accomplish much because God's Kingdom is within us (Luke 17:21). It is fascinating to know that we have the same power that raised Jesus from the dead, living on the inside of us.

However, the first chapter of the book of James reminds us of the power of misplaced words. Eugene Peterson's *The Message* Bible says:

> "*A bit in the mouth of a horse controls the whole horse. A small rudder on a huge ship in the hands of a skilled captain sets a course in the face of the strongest winds. A word out of your mouth may seem of no account, but it can accomplish nearly anything—or destroy it!*" "*It only takes a spark to set off a forest fire. A careless or wrongly placed word out of your mouth can do that. By our speech, we can ruin the world, turn*

harmony into chaos, throw mud on a reputation, send the whole world up in smoke and go up in smoke with it. You can tame a tiger, but you can't tame a tongue. The tongue runs wild, a wanton killer. We bless God our Father; we curse the very men and women he made in his image with the same tongues. Curses and blessings out of the same mouth!" (James 3:3 MSG. Bible)

The old English language children's rhyme says, "Sticks and stones may break my bones, but words will never hurt me." It's a familiar chant from children meaning words can never cause physical pain. I can't express enough the inaccuracy of the statement that words will never hurt. The average broken bone heals within three months, but misspoken words could hurt for an entire lifetime. According to https://mentalhealthdaily.com/, words spoken by a bully are the third leading cause of suicide.

Our sword of the Spirit weapon has the power to destroy or resurrect. Solomon said in Proverbs 16:24 that, "Gracious words are like a honeycomb, sweetness to the soul and health to the body." A sitting United States president's words have the power to impact the economy of three hundred and fifty million people or start a world war. It was fascinating when I came to a knowledge of the truth that our words have the power to re-route storms, dissolve sickness and disease, and change the atmosphere in a room!

The Holy Spirit doing the work

If you are like me and have waited to the last minute to prepare or been caught by surprise by a situation, we must first tame our tongue for maximum results—so much so that Romans chapter eight reminds us we don't often know how to pray as we should, but the Holy Spirit intercedes on behalf of the believers. In my opinion, the eighth chapter of Romans is one of the most misunderstood and misinterpreted chapters in the Bible. Early in my journey, I had an issue with the gift of praying in the Holy Spirit, or tongues, because religion had taught me to reject what I didn't understand. I eventually prayed for understanding, and this is what was revealed to me.

Verse 26 explains how the Holy Spirit helps us when we don't know exactly how to pray about a situation. Have you ever found yourself in a position where you could not find the words to pray? I counseled a family who was having issues with their teenage son. Incarcerated for multiple charges, the most recent one had been driving with an open container in the vehicle. The couple was at odds with what to ask of God. If they prayed for the Lord to release the son from jail, perhaps he would continue drinking and driving and eventually injure himself or someone else seriously. Or, if he remains incarcerated, what if he gets involved with gangs or something worse happens? I did not have an answer to their dilemma, but I recommended they pray in tongues and allow the Spirit to pray to God on their behalf.

The uttering or unspeakable groanings refer to praying in the Holy Spirit or tongues:

> And the Holy Spirit helps us in our weakness. For example, we don't know what God wants us to pray, but the Holy Spirit prays for us with groanings that cannot be expressed in words. (Romans 8:26 NLT).

Jude 1:20-21 confirms that when we pray in tongues, we are "building up ourselves on our most holy faith, praying in the Holy Ghost." In doing so, we keep ourselves in the love of God and confidently trust in Him and His ability.

A practical way to understand the importance of being filled with the Holy Spirit and how the Spirit interceding works is to compare it to a courtroom or the world's law system. In courtrooms of the United States, the parties present in the courtroom are the judge, a jury of twelve, a defendant represented by a defense attorney whose job is to argue and resolve the charges quickly and efficiently, a prosecuting attorney whose job is to bring accusations and present a case he has built against the defendant, witnesses for the defendant and prosecuting attorney, and finally, a stenographer to document the spoken words by all the parties involved.

In closing arguments, the attorney shares case law or common law from previous court cases. The defense attorney pleads on behalf of his client's case laws and general statutes, hopefully proving his client is not guilty. The prosecuting attorney's role is to bring charges against the defendant with evidence so clear that it's beyond a reasonable doubt and convince the jury the defendant is guilty as charged.

In the Kingdom of God system, God is the judge and the Holy Spirit performs the role of a defense attorney making intercessions for us according to the will of God. Satan, the accuser of the brethren, performs the function of a prosecuting attorney who accuses the believers before God. (Revelation 12:10) The angels perform the role of a stenographer, although they only record the perfect prayer between the Holy Spirit and God (Romans 8:26) and go forth to bring it to pass (Psalm 103:20-21).

There is never a jury trial because the believer is always found not guilty based on the Bible Case Law of the Atonement of Jesus Christ. (1 Corinthians 6:7-11) Jesus Himself is the faithful witness for the defendant:

> *"He is the faithful witness to these things, the first to rise from the dead, and the ruler of all the world's kings. All glory to him who loves us and has freed us from our sins by shedding his blood for us."* (Revelations 1:5 NLT)

In our court system, a defendant might not know the case law their defense attorney is sharing with the judge, but they know it is good because the attorney represents them. The couple prayed in tongues on behalf of their incarcerated son, and the Holy Spirit recited Bible Case Law to them.

Perhaps the Spirit was praying this excellent Bible Case Law from the book of Ezekiel on behalf of their son.

> *26 And I will give you a new heart, and I will put a new spirit in you. I will take out your stony, stubborn heart and give you a tender, responsive heart. 27 And I will put my Spirit in you so that you will follow my decrees and be careful to obey my regulations.* (Ezekiel 36:26-27 NLT)

He still prays on your behalf

In the Kingdom of God system, we don't know what the Spirit is praying on our behalf, but we know whatever He's praying is the perfect prayer working in our favor and on our behalf!

> *26 "Likewise the Spirit also helpeth our infirmities: for we know not what we should pray for as we ought: but the Spirit itself maketh intercession for us with groanings which cannot be uttered. (KJV)*
> *27 And he that searcheth the hearts knoweth what is the mind of the Spirit because he maketh intercession for the saints according to the will of God." 28 And we know that all things work together for good to them that love God, to them who are the called according to his purpose.* (Romans 8:26-28 KJV)

I have noted that verses twenty-seven and twenty-eight begin with the conjunction word "And." As you know, this conjunction word functions to join two related statements or comments, such as salt and pepper or peanut butter and jelly. The conjunction word intertwines verses twenty-six to twenty-eight; the writer suggests these scriptures are united, which leads to my theory of the book of Romans chapter eight being one of the most misunderstood passages in the Bible.

It seems to happen without fail when a catastrophe occurs from a car accident, hurricane, tornado, and so on. The family that suffered significant loss will get a call, text, or card that quotes Romans 8:28, "And we know that all things work together for good to those who love God, to those who are the called according to His purpose," because the Bible says so. I am perplexed that a family who lost their nineteen-year-old son to suicide should believe their tragedy is going to "work together for their good."

Chapter Ten

TIMING MEANS EVERYTHING

Like apples of gold, in settings of silver is a word spoken at the proper time. (Proverbs 25:11 NASB)

WE HAVE DEAR friends of more than thirty years who had two children born with neurological disorders that prevented them from speaking or walking at birth and throughout their adult lives. The children could not "work together for the good of the parents" with their conditions. However, they gladly altered their lives and made the best of the situation.

Our friends loved their children and provided the most delicate care that anyone could provide until the day, as adults, they succumbed to their condition and went home to be with the Lord. Many years before their adult children passed, the couple formed a non-profit organization that served as a day program and mental health service for adults. It helped thousands of people over many years and continues to do so today.

I was honored when asked to eulogize at their son's funeral. In the eulogy, I added that their son gets credit for the "assist" of founding the non-profit.

To understand how I could be more sensitive to the needs of bereaving families, I have had many conversations with families several months after their devasting day. I often ask them what was most encouraging and disappointing during their grief. The family usually responds with, "It was encouraging that our circle of support did more listening than trying to explain why this tragedy happened to us," and they did not appreciate people telling them, "It was going to somehow work together for our good because we loved God."

My years of conversation with families recovering from abuse, divorce, or tragedies confirm that Romans 8:28 should never be used independently of verses twenty-five through twenty-seven, which talks about the workings of the Holy Spirit. Could it be that "all things" that are working together for our good are the promises of God found in scriptures? I think of scriptures as "bible case laws" that the Holy Spirit is praying in intercession on our behalf.

We don't know those "things" specific "Bible Case Laws " the Holy Spirit is praying through us, but we know those unknown scriptures are working together for our good because we love the Lord.

Verse twenty-six starts with another connecting word, "likewise," which connects twenty-five and twenty-six:

> [25] *But if we hope for that we see not, then do we wait patiently for it.* [26] *Likewise, the Spirit also helpeth our infirmities: for we know not what we should pray for as we ought: but the Spirit itself maketh intercession for us with groanings which cannot be uttered.* (Romans 8:25 KJV)

The thought comes to mind of a pregnant woman awaiting the arrival of a baby she can't see but knows something is happening inside her. Her tone changes from "we're believing for a baby," to "We're expecting!" She hopes for what she can't see, and waits patiently while enduring months of fatigue, headaches, mood swings, and morning sickness. And, when the baby arrives, the joy overwhelms her pain. If you've found yourself in a position you can't see your way out of, you must hope for the thing you can't see. When hope against hope is gone, we hope in faith, and we know that God is faithful and always true to His promises and can be depended on.

At a loss for words

Many years ago, I made a couple of investments that did not turn out as planned. The worst-case scenarios in both vested interests happened to us. We had a financial dilemma and could not see our way out. The Greek meaning of the word dilemma is "double proposition." We found ourselves having to choose between two unfavorable options.

As a result, it causes us to lose sleep and feel overwhelmed. In addition, we could not find the right words to pray about our situation. As much as we tried, the words would not come. It was as if we had temporary brain fog. Perhaps you have experienced what we were experiencing, feelings of helplessness and despair. We said, "Lord, we don't know what to pray or what to do." We then sat for a while until the Lord interrupted our silence and told us to pray in tongues.

After praying in tongues for the next hour, I asked the Lord to give me an interpretation of what the Holy Spirit was praying through me. The scripture 1 Corinthians 10:13 NLT immediately came to mind:

> *"The temptations in your life are no different from what others experience. And God is faithful. He will not allow the temptation to be more than you can stand. When you are tempted, he will show you a way out so you can endure."* (1 Corinthians 10:13 NLT)

The scripture reassures our hearts that God is not the culprit behind any trouble that comes our way. He said He would not allow the temptation to be more than we can stand, and He would show us a way out, so we can continue in the same state without quitting or giving up. If he desired to tempt you or for you to suffer, He would not have said He's providing a way out. As I prayed in tongues, I believed the Holy Spirit presented this Bible Case Law to God on our behalf. At that moment, I imagined Him saying, "My Lord, they are your faithful servants, and You said that the temptation they are going through is common to man, but You said when temptations come, you would show them a way out." Your servants need Your wisdom and unearned favor right now."

The Lord gave us the wisdom to overcome the financial dilemma. However, deliverance did not come overnight in this situation; within a few months; we resolved the difficulty without going to the bank for a loan. Praise God! Undoubtedly, that "Bible Case Law" the Holy Spirit prayed on our behalf worked together for our good! The right word at the right time means everything.

Chapter Eleven

Do Common Things Uncommonly Well

EPHESIANS 6:16-17 SAYS in the *New American Standard Bible* that, with "the shield of faith," we will be able to extinguish flaming arrows of the evil one; And we take the Shield of Faith and our Sword of the Spirit, by "speaking the words of God." As we thrive on being "imitators of God," it is essential to remember that the Lord does not respond to emotions. He only responds to the believer's faith that has taken authority over the situation.

As we were going through our financial dilemma, the Lord did not respond because we were emotional. He did not respond until we took charge of those emotions. It is essential to know that we do not live with our decisions but their consequences. Yes, we are emotional creatures and sometimes make hasty decisions from negative emotions. We can decide quickly, but the results could last weeks, months, or even years. The Old Testament recorded the Israel children's journey and was written for our instructions.

> *¹¹ Now these things befell them by way of a figure [as an example and warning to us]; they were written to admonish and fit us for right action by good instruction, we in whose days the ages have reached their climax (their consummation and concluding period).* (1 Corinthians 10:11 AMPC)

The book of Deuteronomy 1 records Moses's address to the people of Israel forty years after they departed Egypt. He said it was an eleven-day journey to the promised land, yet it took them forty years to get there. Imagine that you and your family were traveling from the West Coast to the East Coast by vehicle and expected to arrive in several days; instead, it took you forty years to get there. One thing I've noted about how an eleven-day journey became a forty-year journey was the words of ten of the twelve spies that brought back an evil report of the land. (Numbers 13:32)

Despite what the Lord had said, the spies claimed the land was a death trap, and they could not take it. Without asking any further questions, the entire community received the report as the gospel by the end of the day. They became very emotional and cried all night. (Numbers 14:1 NKJV) The next day, they grumbled and complained against Moses, Aaron, and the Lord. They said, *"Why has the Lord has brought us to this land to die by the sword."* *And they said to one another, "We will choose captains and return to Egypt?"* (Numbers 14:3-4 NKJV)

They never considered that the Lord parted the Red Sea and provided manna from heaven to bring them to where they were standing. Yet, they planned to return to Egypt without His help. Every Jewish family had received gold and jewelry from the Egyptians during the night of the Passover.

Furthermore, the Egyptians' firstborn died that very night, and out of their emotions, the Jews apparently assumed that Pharaoh would throw them a welcome home party once they returned. Their story proves that emotional people make bad decisions as it was with the Israelites. I have watched suspense movies that have kept me on the edge of my seat in fear, and once the movie is over, my heart is still racing as if it happened. That is how it is with our emotions. They will only follow how we're feeling at that moment.

Zig Ziglar once said, "Fear is a great inhibitor of performance. We were born to win, but to be a winner, plan, prepare and expect to win." Brainyquote. com. They did not expect to win.

Their results explain why paying attention to details and taking care of the little things, such as "harnessing our negative emotions," is of the utmost importance.

John D. Rockefeller once said, "The secret of success is to do the common things uncommonly well." Goodreads.com. At sermonillustrations.com, the story was told about the legendary NBA coach Pat Riley. He coached the Los Angeles Lakers for eight years, beginning in 1982. Under Riley, the team won an impressive four championships! How did Riley do it? He explained his success in two practical points:

#1. He said that he understood success is often achieved through the little stuff.

#2. He noted that his talent lies in his ability to pay attention to detail. For example, he pointed out that every NBA team studies film and compiles statistics to evaluate players' game performances. However, Riley used those tools more comprehensively than his rivals.

Riley said, "Instead of focusing on baskets made, blocked shots, and rebounds, we measure areas of performance that are often ignored such as jumping in pursuit of every rebound even if you do not get it, swatting at every pass even if you do not touch the ball, diving for loose balls even if you are not successful, and letting someone smash into you to draw a foul, even if the charge foul is not called." After each game, that is what we called measuring "effort," Riley said. Furthermore, those statistics were punched into a computer.

"Effort" and taking care of the little stuff "is what ultimately separates journeyman players (who is reliable but not outstanding) from impact players (who are reliable and outstanding, making their presence felt and profound). Knowing how well a player executes all the little stuff is the key to unlocking career-best performances," Riley explained. Like the coach, we should often ask ourselves how well we are with taking care of the little stuff and doing everyday things uncommonly well, like harnessing our negative emotions.

Another little fox that spoils the vines is negative emotions. Like Solomon and Pat Riley, I have learned that life is about taking care of the little things. Words spoken out of emotions have aborted destinies, ended marriages, and torn families apart.

In the court of law, if an individual giving testimony under oath is overcome with emotions, the judge will often call for a recess to give that person time to bring their feelings under control before testimony resumes. At the height of our emotional times, we should consider a reprieve. Moreover, Jesus reminds us that when we pray, we should not go on repeating words emotionally as if we will be heard through much repetition.

> *"And when you come before God, do not turn that into a theatrical production. These people make a regular show out of their prayers, hoping for fifteen minutes of fame! Do you think God sits in a box seat? Here is what I want you to do: Find a quiet, secluded place so you will not be tempted to role-play before God. Just be there as simply and honestly as you can manage. The focus will shift from you to God, and you will begin to sense his grace."* (Matthew 6:5-6 MSG. Bible).

In the Old Testament, David found himself in a difficult emotional situation. He and his men had traveled three days to return home to Ziklag, only to find that the Amalekites had raided their homes, burned down the entire city, and taken their wives and children captive. We can appreciate David and his men who were overcome with grief. Imagine the men traveling as fast as they could to make it home. They were motivated by the thoughts of hugging their wives and children and then enjoying a good family meal. However, everything they had worked so hard for was gone instantly. The men wept until they had no more tears to cry. They began pointing fingers at those whom they thought were to blame for their emotional outburst. All the men, in unison, blamed David for their horrific loss.

Slowing down to hear His voice

The men were bitter and talked of stoning David. After David had controlled his emotions, he asked the priest to bring the sacred garment, and he prayed to God. "Shall I go after this gang of rebels? If I do, will I catch them?" Furthermore, God answered, "Yes. Go after them, and you will not only catch them but recover everything taken from you and your men." It is worth noting that David did not try to make a spiritual connection with the Lord until he had gotten over his emotions. If you were in a situation where you only had two days to make a decision, it would be more beneficial for you to use the first day praying in the spirit and then listening for an answer during the second day.

Perhaps David understood that praying amid his emotions would hinder him from hearing the voice of the Lord. David and four hundred men pursued the raiders, overcame them, and recovered it all, just as the word of the Lord had promised. (1 Samuel 30:1-20) David's success depended on his ability to tame his emotions and tune himself to hear from God. The priest brought the sacred garment, and David sought God wholeheartedly. Working together, David and the priest got an answer to their prayers.

In the book of Isaiah, the story is recorded of Hezekiah, the king of Judah. After receiving a letter from the evil King Sennacherib, he laid the letter before God and prayed.

> Hezekiah prayed to the Lord, saying, "O Lord of hosts, the God of Israel, who is enthroned above the cherubim, You are the God, You alone, of all the kingdoms of the earth. You have made heaven and earth.

Incline Your ear, O Lord, and hear; open Your eyes, O Lord, and see; and listen to all the words of Sennacherib, who sent them to reproach the living God. Truly, O Lord, the kings of Assyria have devastated all the countries and their lands, and have cast their gods into the fire, for they were not gods but the work of men's hands, wood, and stone. So, they have destroyed them. Now, O Lord our God, deliver us from his hand that all the kingdoms of the earth may know that You alone, Lord, are God." (Isaiah 37:15-20) (Source: https://bible.knowing-jesus.com)

Isaiah prayed that his people would be delivered from the evil king and that all the kingdoms of the earth may know that God alone is Lord over the globe. It is still God's will that every nation knows that He's God and there's none other. By doing so, he prayed for the perfect will of God in his situation, and the Lord answered his request overnight.

Chapter Twelve

PRAYING WITH CONFIDENCE

MORE THAN THIRTY years ago, researchers experimented to see the effect of hope on those undergoing hardships. Two sets of laboratory mice were placed in separate tubs of water. The researchers left one set in the water and found that they had all drowned within an hour. The other mice were periodically lifted out of the water and then returned. When that happened, the second set of mice swam for over twenty-four hours. Why? It is not because they were given a rest, but because they suddenly had hope!

Those mice somehow hoped that someone would reach down and rescue them if they could stay afloat just a little longer. If hope holds such power for unthinking rodents, how much more significant should its effect be on our lives? (Source: sermonillustrations.com)

Webster's 1828 dictionary defines confidence as a trusting assurance of mind and a firm belief in the integrity, stability, or honesty of another. The sixteenth century Martin Luther once said, "The creator of all things has made all things depend on faith so that whoever has faith will have everything, and whoever does not have faith will have nothing."

A prayer of doubt, unbelief, and uncertainty is like cutting a link out of a bicycle chain, causing dysfunction. When there is an emergency, most people send an urgent 911 prayer request to their Facebook friends and start a prayer chain with strangers. It is perfectly okay to do that. But, we feel it is essential for us to know what the people who are praying on our behalf during a crisis believe. Perhaps they are "making a regular show of their prayers, or hoping for fifteen minutes of fame?" Maybe they are praying, "If it is your will, God?" We understand that it only takes two people praying and believing in harmony to get the job done! We often keep our significant prayer needs and concerns between mature prayer intercessors.

We love sharing the joy of an answered prayer, especially with those that have stood in the gap with us. They become more confident as the good news spreads. Finding prayer partners, elders, or deacons with a proven track record of getting spiritual breakthroughs is essential. The prayer partners must understand how to pray confidently and not wonder if it's God's will; they find the will of God in the scriptures and pray for His will over the crisis. (1 John 5:14-15)

I know some people will say this way of thinking is extreme or unnecessary. However, if you were looking for an investment broker, would it be extreme for you to ask the brokers what their average return on investment (ROI) is for their clients? And, while looking for a realtor to sell a home, would it be unnecessary to search for an individual with a proven track record of multiple recent sales? We strategically choose physicians, barbers, hair stylists, dry cleaning companies, and even restaurants. How much more should we strategically choose prayer partners in a possible life or death situation?

Jesus reminds us that our Sword of the Spirit has the power to bind, confine, restrain, and restrict as it is in heaven, and it allows us to set things free as it is in heaven. Jesus withered the fig tree by saying, "No one will eat from you again!" Furthermore, we should be imitators and speak to the Goliaths in our lives that need to be bound, confined, and withered.

As it is in heaven

We speak to those things seemingly held up in prayer to be loosed and free in Jesus's name! However, as previously mentioned, prayer does not require many friends and strangers. It seems the unspoken rule is, "The Lord will *only* respond if enough people come together and pray." However, Jesus said in Matthew 18:19 (NKJV), "If two of you agree on earth concerning anything they ask, it will be done for them by My Father in heaven."

Matthew 18:18 in the *Amplified Bible (Classic Edition)* says, "Truly I tell you, whatever you forbid and declare to be improper and unlawful on earth must be what is already forbidden in heaven, and whatever you permit and declare proper and lawful on earth must be what is already permitted in heaven."

Tarsha's grandmother was a devout Christian and a relatively healthy lady. However, she had sudden complications one day in the emergency room. She was moved from the ER to a critical care unit after the medical team confirmed she had congestive heart failure. Moreover, she was put on a life-support machine for the next few days, giving her very unfavorable odds of surviving.

We were at the hospital having a conversation. We discussed whether her grandmother was ready to transition to heaven. Tarsha said things had happened so fast, and Grandma had no opportunity to say goodbye to everyone. We agreed to pray for the restoration of her internal organs. We kindly asked some family members if we could have a few private minutes with Grandma, and they obliged. It was important for the two of us to privately pray over Grandma because a few of the family members present were unbelievers.

We stood on Matthew 18:18, "congestive heart failure is forbidden in heaven," and we declared it forbidden over Grandma. We decreed restoration to her internal organs and that her heart will pump blood as efficiently as created to do, in Jesus' name! After we prayed, the family returned to the bedside.

However, there was no immediate change to her condition. Shortly afterward, the medical team disconnected Grandma from the life support system. She lay on the bed, gasping for air. Her short, quick breaths signified that it was only a matter of time until she expired. However, those short quick breaths soon turned into slow and controlled breathing. After checking her vitals and recognizing her condition was reversing itself, the physicians were in awe on that joyful Sunday night when her organs became alive and kicking again! The following Wednesday, the medical team determined that her vitals were normal, and they approved a discharge from the hospital.

Grandma made a complete recovery within a few days. One week after her discharge, she was driving once again! Praise God! Grandma recovered because we stood on Matthew 18:18-19, and the Lord honored His Word. We believed that Jesus meant what He said, and Grandma returned to life.

It is essential not to be moved with emotions when there is no visible improvement after praying about a situation. If someone prays over an aching body part, and they still have the pain afterward, do not be moved with emotions. It is okay to ask a person to do something they couldn't do before after you finish praying for them, but it's unnecessary to pray over and over until they tell you they're healed to get you to stop pressuring them even though they feel the same.

Transitioning from the "AHA" moments of life

Jesus gave us a command in Mark 11:24 (NKJV). Jesus said; "Therefore I say to you, whatever things you ask when you pray, believe...."

He did not say that when you pray, only believe if there is no pain, or when praying, only consider that healing has manifested if the physician confirms the tumor is gone. Paul warned us "be not conformed" to the world's system, where it must "be seen to be believed." In God's system, "we believe it when we speak His Word" to see it manifest!

In Mark 11:14 (NASB), Jesus cursed the fig tree because it was covered with leaves from a distance, and he assumed that it would be full of figs, but he found nothing but leaves even though it was the season for figs. However, no change happened in the natural world as observed by seeing, and the tree was deteriorating in its roots the very moment Jesus spoke. The verse ends with an intriguing statement:

> *"And He said to it, 'May no one ever eat fruit from you again!'*
> *And His disciples were listening."* (Mark 11:14 NASB)

His disciples were not saying anything or giving Jesus a big "Amen!" They did not see anything happening in the natural, so they did not respond. Perhaps Jesus cursing the fig tree was a faith class for his disciples. Jesus taught his disciples to believe when they say it, not when they see it. I could imagine that when those disciples were by themselves, they could have been saying things like, "Hey fellows, can you believe Jesus was talking to a tree?" "He must have been starving." As we "imitate" Jesus and follow His example, we speak to cancer, trauma, tumor, evil spirits, and pain in the name of Jesus! "

Talk to your problem about your God

Knowledge will teach us to transition from speaking to God about our problems to talking directly to our problems about our God!"

The following day when they passed by the fig tree that Jesus had cursed, Peter exclaimed, *"The fig tree you cursed has withered away!"* Peter had an "AHA" moment with God. An AHA moment happens when we are surprised that Jesus did what he said he would do. That AHA moment proved their lack of confidence in His trustworthiness.

We should not be surprised when we get an answer to prayers. Being appreciative, grateful, and excited that someone came to the rescue differs from being surprised that they showed up to do what they had promised. We can measure faith's maturity by those AHA moments. Children have AHA

---

moments when Mom and Dad promise ice cream and deliver. *"Mom and Dad, I can't believe you did this for me!"*

1 Corinthians 13:11 (AMPC) explains it this way: *"When I was a child, I talked like a child, I thought like a child, I reasoned like a child; now that I have become a man, I am done with childish ways and have put them aside."*

For better results, consume it like your daily vitamins

The sons and daughters of Abraham research the scriptures for an answer to a situation or circumstance, and once they find it, they meditate on it day and night. They consume it like their daily vitamins and believe it will make their way prosperous even before it manifests in the natural world. Before and after it manifests itself physically, they praise the Lord, the giver of all good and perfect gifts!

Several years ago, I was at my dentist's office for a minor procedure. The dental assistant made small talk with me as we waited in the procedure room for the dentist. After answering her questions about my family, I asked about hers. I noticed her countenance change, and she explained that she and her husband had tried for more than ten years to have a child before giving up. She continued to tell me why every physician they visited told her she could not conceive. As she started sharing medical terms well beyond my comprehension, I interrupted her and asked if she still wanted to have a child. She said they would love to have a child if there were any way medically possible. I told her that I didn't know of a way medically, but God's word had her "Yes" answer. Before the doctor entered, I asked her to quickly grab a pen and paper and write two scriptures down.

> [14] *This is the confidence which we have before Him, that, if we ask anything according to His will, He hears us.* [15] *And if we know that He hears us in whatever we ask, we know that*

we have the requests which we have asked from Him. (1 John 5:14-15 NASB)

[11] *For the Lord God is a sun and shield; The Lord gives grace and glory; He withholds no good thing from those who walk with integrity.* (Psalm 84:11 NASB)

I prayed these scriptures over her and instructed her to recite these as if she were taking vitamins the first thing in the morning, at noontime, and nightly before she went to sleep. In doing so, she would remind herself that when she feels inadequate, she's relying on her confidence in Him and not herself. In addition, she agreed with her husband that having a child would be a good thing, and the scripture said that He would not withhold "no good thing." When I returned for a six-month check-up, she was pregnant. After she gave me a big hug, she said she conceived about three weeks after taking her prescription scriptures. Praise God! She continued to express her gratitude for the prayer and scriptures I shared, but I interrupted her once again to say, "You conceived according to your faith." She took the word and feasted upon it for three weeks. The consistent meditation changed her thought life.

Over a decade ago, a trend spread throughout the United States. Individuals expressed themselves with two words on bumper stickers and rear window decals of their primary activity. If a family had kids playing soccer, the decal would read, "Soccer Life, or for the beachgoer, "Beach Life." I believe that, for a person that desires to have success and enjoy good days whether apparent or not, their primary activity should be controlling their "Thought Life." As you think, so are you. My friend changed her thinking and produced her offspring. The word of God makes the impossible possible!

Chapter Thirteen

MAKE THE MOST
OF AN OPPORTUNITY

THE NINETEENTH CENTURY comedian, actor, and Broadway performer Will Rogers was known for his wit and common-sense attitude, making him one of the world's most famous actors and comedians. We could compare him to Jerry Seinfeld or Kevin Hart because of his ability to entertain and make people laugh.

On one occasion, Will Rogers entertained at the former Milton H. Berry Institute in L.A. This hospital rehabilitates polio victims, people with broken backs, and other extreme physical handicaps. Of course, Rogers had everybody laughing, even patients in appalling conditions, but then he abruptly left the platform and raced to the restroom. His assistant followed to give him a towel and when he opened the door, he saw Rogers leaning against the wall sobbing uncontrollably like a little child. Rogers had been gazing into the audience at the extreme physical handicaps.

The assistant immediately closed the door, and Rogers returned to the platform in a few minutes as cheerful as before. Here is an old saying that still stands true today: "If you want to learn what a person is really like, ask three questions: What makes them laugh? What makes them upset? Furthermore, what causes them to weep like a child?" Moreover, these are relatively good tests of character questions that are especially appropriate for leaders.

Many people say, "We need angry leaders today!" "The time has come to practice militant Christianity!" However, the excellent book reminds us that "man's anger does not promote the righteousness or justice God [wishes and requires]."

Warren Wiersbe once said that "what we need today is not anger but anguish." It is that kind of anguish that Moses displayed when he broke the two tablets of the law, *and then* he climbed the mountain to intercede for the people, or that anguish Jesus expressed when He cleansed the temple, kicking over tables and throwing out everyone who had set up their shops for buying and selling after which He poured out his heart and wept over the city. The difference between anger and anguish is a broken heart, a spirit crushed over sin and injustice. (Source: sermonillustrations.com)

I have discovered that anger and anguish are cousins. Moreover, it is easy to invite cousin anger into our home. Yet, it is a little more challenging to have the "and then" cousin anguish as a permanent guest in our lives.

Allow anguish to lead the way when using your Sword of the Spirit for prayer when you speak with non-believers; we should conduct ourselves with wisdom toward outsiders, making the most of the opportunity. Furthermore, ensure that our speech is always with grace, as though seasoned with salt, so we will know how to respond to each person. (Colossians 5)

We were in Hilo, Hawai'i, praying with a family for their husband who was involved in an all-terrain vehicle (ATV) accident. I observed a man who was part of the facility staff as he watched the family praying and calling out to God. He had a puzzled demeanor as if to say, "What are these people doing, and why are they wasting their time doing it?" Before we left the facility, the Lord set up private time between us, and I knew that I had to make the most of this brief opportunity.

After we introduced ourselves, I thanked him for the care he and his organization provided for the family. After a few minutes of small talk, we discussed his thoughts on this family's prayer time for their loved one. He said he had no views or opinions about it because he was an atheist. He shared that his parents practiced Islam as a kid and later started practicing Buddhism. A few years afterward, his parents gave up on their religions. By the time he became a teenager, he had developed an absence of belief in the existence of any deity. As he continued speaking, the thought in my mind was, "Lord, I need something supernatural to happen if you desire for me to reach this man."

When he finished, I explained to him that I believed in God and His Son Jesus, that died, resurrected, and gave every believer His Holy Spirit to navigate them through life. At that very moment, the Holy Spirit gave me a Word of Knowledge to share with him. After asking for permission to share, I shared that he had been perplexed and lost lots of sleep over the past few months. I told him that I saw a vision of him sitting up in bed in the middle of the night as if he had had a bad dream. Furthermore, the dream continued to happen nightly and week after week. In addition, I told him his troubles were concerning a huge life transition. His demeanor changed as I was giving this Word of Knowledge. It was as if the strength had left his body, with a pale face and eyes twice as big as regular size. He just stirred into my face for a couple of minutes that seemed like fifteen.

He said that his girlfriend's family lived out west in the United States; he agreed to transition from Hilo to the mainland to live with her parents for a while. He had plans to work with her father, but he feared things would not pan out. His horrifying dreams were that he had transitioned and sold his home, but things did not work out with the job or relationship. He said he often panicked in the middle of the night after dreaming that he had lost everything and become homeless.

He added that he was thirty years old and had never left the Big Island of Hawai'i. I asked a simple question: "Do you think I could have known unless the Holy Spirit told me?" He said, "There is no way you could have known because I have never shared this with anyone." I told him that if he received Christ as His Savior, the Holy Spirit would not only navigate him through his current situation but all the ones to come. He said that he wanted to receive my God as his God. Praise God! His nightmares were partly true. A life without Christ is an empty life of helplessness and homelessness, but the Love of Christ living in the believer will never fail.

Faith that guarantees great results

We discussed in the "living in the bubble" chapter that when anything negative happens, the believer should decree, "That is not from God!" The problem with believing the Lord had a part to play in their misfortune, or that of a friend or family member, is that the God needed to help them overcome is the same God they believe had something to do with the mishap or adverse circumstance. It is impossible to confidently ask someone to rescue us from our misfortune if we believe they are the culprit behind our trouble.

As a reminder, according to the apostle John, the prerequisite to the answered prayer is being confident that the Lord has our "Yes" answer because we asked according to His will. (1 John 5:14-15) The Faith we have is in Him and not ourselves. In addition, accidents happen when there are violations of spiritual and natural laws. If someone decides to jump off a tall building, the law of gravity will always work against them.

Although, jumping with a parachute will regulate the law of gravity. The Airbus Superjumbo seats five hundred and fifty passengers and weighs six hundred tons when fully loaded. The captain cannot boast how he caused the machine to fly; the engineers were obedient to design and carefully construct it within the laws of gravity and aerodynamics. Laws regulate the earth, and when we work within the Laws of his word, good things happen for us; we should never boast or brag because it is what the Spirit is doing through us and not our own.

God asked Job if he knew the ordinances (regulations) of the universe and can he use them to control the earth; could he shout to the clouds and make it rain? (Job 38:33-34) The answer is always yes for the believer who believes that God can do exceedingly, abundantly above all they could ask, think, or imagine beyond their wildest dreams, according to the power that works within them! (Ephesians 3:20)

The prophet Elijah was an excellent example of going to battle and not having everything he needed, but he discovered his "faith words" were more than enough to regulate the Earth. Elijah answered yes to the question of regulating the Earth with his faith. Although it had not rained for three and a half years, Elijah prayed (shouted to the clouds), and rain returned to the Earth. (1 Kings 18:45) How did Elijah regulate the Earth? He believed that what God said would come to pass.

God commanded Elijah to show himself to King Ahab, and He would send rain upon the Earth. (1 Kings 18:1) It was not a simple task for Elijah to show himself. Ahab and Jezebel had accused Elijah of the forty-two months of drought, and they would not be excited to see him. Like Elijah, faith's destiny is for us to move toward the unknown. Your provision is on the other side of your greatest fear: your supply and those connected to you. I can only imagine the onslaught of attacks Satan unleashed on Elijah while on his way to meet Ahab at Mount Carmel to pray for rain.

I can imagine the burden of mental and emotional attacks that came one after another. "Who do you think you are!?" "It has not rained in three and a half years; why do you think you can make a difference?" "What will people think if you fail?" "Ahab and Jezebel will have your head on a platter." "What if you misunderstood God?" "What if it does not work out?" We can easily discern whether the Holy Spirit or the devil is speaking to us. Evil spirits are known to torment believers and unbelievers with the thoughts of "what if." The Holy Spirit searches deep and knows the end of things from its beginning. Therefore, He would never ask the what-if question. All His promises are yes and amen! In Psalm 89, Ethan the Ezrahite sings a song of God's binding contract:

> ³ [You have said] I have made a covenant with My chosen one, I have sworn to David, My servant. ³³ Nevertheless, My loving-kindness will I not break off from him, nor allow My faithfulness to fail [to lie and be false to him]. ³⁴ My covenant will I not break or profane, nor alter the thing that is gone out of My lips. ³⁵ Once [for all] have I sworn by My holiness, which cannot be violated; I will not lie to David. (Psalm 89:3,33-35 AMPC)

A facility, home, the constitution, and our appearance can be altered or entirely changed. Still, the things that God has spoken are impossible to be varied to any degree.

Elijah understood that what God had said was an unchangeable promise. That is why the enemy's voice did not cause Elijah to waiver or doubtingly question because he believed that God was able to keep His word—"Go show yourself to King Ahab, and I will send rain." (1 Kings 18:1 NKJV). Elijah was on top of Mount Carmel with his servant, bowed down with his head between his knees, praying. I can imagine that Elijah was giving God His word back in his prayers. "Lord, you said if I show myself to King Ahab, you will send the rain." Although it had not rained in more than three years, I can imagine that Elijah was thanking the Lord for the rain.

The servant looks over the mountain across the sea six times only to report that nothing is out there. Furthermore, Elijah continued to thank God for His promise of rain. In everything, give thanks to the Lord. I am not thankful "for" negative things happening in my life, but "in" the middle of those things, I choose to give the Lord thanks. According to His word, He will deliver me out of every affliction. I have decided to sing like Ethan the Ezrahite:

> *¹ I will sing of the mercy and loving-kindness of the Lord for-ever; with my mouth will I make known Your faithfulness from generation to generation. ² For I have said, Mercy and loving-kindness shall be built up forever; Your faithfulness will You establish in the very heavens [unchangeable and perpetual].* (Psalm 89:1-2 AMPC)

On the seventh time, the servant saw a cloud the size of a man's hand. Although the outward condition or circumstance had not changed, Elijah told his servant to get off the mountain because he heard an abundance of rain.

> *"Now Faith is the Substance of things hoped for, the evidence of things not seen."* (Hebrews 11:1 NKJV)

Notice the scripture "does not say" that faith is the evidence of things that do not exist but the evidence of things not seen. What we pray "according to God's will," it does exist and must be seen first spiritually. I like to think of faith as a QR Code. As you know, speed is the primary benefit of the code, hence why it's named a Quick Response code. The QR code is designed to allow the user to access data quickly. Faith is designed to grant the user quick access to the supernatural, miracles, and answered prayers. Elijah was praying according to God's will and used his faith to gain access to the supernatural world.

Soon afterward, the sky was full of dark rain clouds and poured abundant rain to replenish the Earth. Faith is Substance (real, tangible, not imaginary). Elijah could see what the natural eyes could not see, and the natural ears could not hear. Before Elijah prayed, he told Ahab that he could hear an abundance of rain.

> *⁴¹ Then Elijah said to Ahab, "Go up, eat and drink; for there is the sound of abundance of rain." ⁴² So Ahab went up to eat and drink. And Elijah went up to the top of Carmel; then he bowed down on the ground, and put his face between his knees, ⁴³ and said to his servant, "Go up now, look toward the sea."* 1 Kings 18:41-43 (NKJV).

Many people depended on Elijah's faith not to fail him. The rain meant life, income, freedom, and deliverance for the entire country. Elijah's Shield of Faith was the word (the promise) that God had given him.

What you have is more than enough

Perhaps you have heard the true story of Ms. Georgene Johnson, who had gotten to the starting line fifteen minutes too early. However, the mistake cost her twenty miles and a pair of aching knees, but she said the following Monday morning that she was happy with the outcome. At that time, the forty-two-year-old secretary was slated to run a 10-K race on Sunday morning. Instead, she mistakenly joined about four-thousand runners taking part in a marathon. Rather than quit, she hung on to finish the twenty-six-mile race. "As stupid as I felt out there running, I am proud of myself," Johnson said in a Monday morning interview. "I guess I was in better shape than I thought. I feel fine, although my knees are sore this morning." The 10K race started at 8:45 am. However, the marathon started fifteen minutes earlier. Moreover, both races used the same starting line.

Four miles down the road, as the route left downtown and moved into residential areas, she said, "I got that sick feeling that possibly I was in the wrong race." Another runner confirmed her suspicions. However, Johnson finished the marathon in an impressive four hours and four minutes, good enough for eighty-third place in the women's division. Before the twenty-six-mile marathon, her previous longest run was only eight miles. Wow! (Source: sermonillustrations.com)

I do not know about you, but I have had times like Georgene, that sick feeling like I am in over my head and "in the wrong race." Nevertheless, it was the best thing that could have ever happened to me, being over my head. Instead of trusting in my strength and wits to get me out, I was forced to trust in God.

Perhaps Satan has waged a mental and emotional war on you with similar questions that he bombarded on Elijah. Moreover, you are feeling over-whelmed with those thoughts. Furthermore, like Georgene, we will discover that we are more robust and in better shape than we thought. Although we may not have everything we need for the battles we are in and the ones to come, we will soon discover that our spiritual weapons are just enough to be victorious!

We have the Shield of Faith (God's promises) at our disposal to quench those fiery darts that attempt to inflict a disabling wound. The Shield of Faith is for extinguishing those fiery darts of evil. No matter what comes your way, do not lay down your Shield. It is impossible to please God without it, and He rewards those that choose to hold on to it. (Hebrews 11:6) The word God spoke to Elijah became law, and God's word will never return void.

Chapter Fourteen

FAITH WORDS AT WORK

LET US NOT soon forget that young David fighting his Goliath (his massive problem) with five smooth stones and a slingshot has taught us that sometimes we go to battle without everything we need. If we follow God's plan, He will help us use our invisible weapons to deal wisely and succeed. The woman who had the twelve-year blood issue has taught us that our words have power. She changed her thinking and speaking.

> *28 For she kept saying, If I only touch His garments, I shall be restored to health.* (Mark 5:28 AMPC)

She touched him and was made completely whole, "*34 And He said to her, "Daughter, your faith has made you well. Go in peace, and be healed of your affliction."* (Mark 5:34 NKJV)

Have you ever wondered why we are still talking about a woman with no other name but a "certain woman" that lived two thousand years ago? The dictionary defines "certain" as special, beyond doubt, or specific. If a "specific" woman had an issue, it leads one to believe that she was not the only woman on that day that had problems and the same issue. However, He singled out this "specific" woman.

Let me explain in another way. When choosing a pet, we prefer a "certain or specific" one. We visited the kennel many years ago to select our Mini Australian Shepherd puppy. The breeder said, "Okay, choose the one you want." There were some black ones, brown ones, black and white ones, but only one red one. We said almost simultaneously, "We want that one!" "The Mini Red!" They were all Mini Australian Shepards, but our Sadie was exceptional.

A few things made this woman exceptional, specific, or unique. She had suffered trauma at the hands of many physicians. Due to her blood loss, she was more than likely constantly anemic, dizzy, and weak. Perhaps she was confused and bombarded with anxiety and uneasiness. The symptoms were magnified due to the thoughts and feelings of being uncleaned. She was treated as ceremonially unclean. (Leviticus 15) Anyone who touched her during that time was considered unclean, and anything she felt became unclean.

We do not know if she had a husband and children but, if she did, she would not have been able to hug them or sleep in the same bed with her husband. In addition, she was not able to attend community gatherings. To make matters worse, she had been forced to social distance herself for twelve years. She was socially distanced from society and perhaps her family for more than four thousand days and never gave up on getting healed. She was indeed an exceptional, specific, and extraordinary woman beyond doubt.

She had heard a report concerning Jesus. We are not sure what she heard about Jesus, perhaps that others had touched His garment and all who touched Him were made perfectly whole. (Matthew 14:35-36 KJV) *"For she kept saying, If I only touch His garments, I shall be restored to health."* (Mark 5:28 AMPC). This woman risked it all to get her healing. She was required to shout out loud, "Unclean!" "Unclean!" when she was in public.

However, she pressed her way through the crowd risking everything to get close to Jesus. She thought, "He does not have to look at me, acknowledge me, nor speak to me; if I can get close enough to touch that garment, my twelve-year Goliath will end today!" When she touched Him, she felt within herself that the condition that kept her in bondage for twelve long years had dried up from its roots. When Jesus felt within Himself that virtue (power and anointing) had left His body, He turned to see the woman who touched Him. After her explanation, He told the "special" woman that her faith had made her whole. Yes, she upheld the "Shield of Faith" and overcame!

Chosen Royal is your new name

This woman was so unique that a name like Linda, Patty, Lisa, or Shirley was not good enough. Her birth-given name did not cut it! Furthermore, He has given you a name greater than your birth name. He said,

> *"But you are a chosen people, a royal priesthood, a holy nation, a people for God's possession, so that you may proclaim the excellencies of Him who has called you out of darkness into His marvelous light."* (1 Peter 2:9 NASB).

Chosen is your first name, and your surname is Royal. You are Chosen Royal, and He wants you to proclaim His Glorious Praises! He desires that you be whole in Spirit, Soul, and Body.

Paul gave a charge to the church (soldiers) of Ephesus to:

"Stand therefore, having girded your waist with truth, having put on the breastplate of righteousness." (Ephesians 6:14 NKJV)

The translation of "girded" literally means to "bind by surrounding." God's word is truth, and we should surround ourselves with it as if we were putting on a belt. A belt serves the purpose of holding everything together.

Discover the hidden truths among numerous options

Throughout our educational career, we have learned that studying and understanding the answers is the key to success during the big exam day.

Deception by multiple choice is not a problem when we have reviewed and understood the answers. The truth hides within numerous options. As we know, life gives us various decisions. Moreover, the Word of God provides us with the solution for every one of life's problems.

Jesus explained this point to His disciples in John 8:31-32. He told the Jews who believed in Him that if they continued in His word, they were His disciples and would know the truth, making them accessible. Faith comes by hearing and hearing and hearing the word of God. We should be cautious about the thought and studies we give toward what we hear. It determines the measure of power and knowledge returned to us.

Joshua referred to God's word as the book of the law. He exclaimed that this law book should never depart from our mouths, but we should meditate on it day and night so that we may comply with its instructions. Only then would we make our way prosperous, deal wisely, and have success. (Joshua 1:8) A rotisserie keeps the meat turning slowly and constantly as it cooks. Joshua has given us the recipe for success: to meditate, "to think calm thoughts, and let the word turn slowly and constantly in our mind." The word must be marinated within our hearts.

The first three words of the original Constitution of the United States created in 1787 are, "We the People." According to the International Idea Institute, "Our Constitution is a book of laws created to take care of the fundamental things we need, such as security and protection from violence as well as the opportunity for success through education." According to Jesus, the Bible, the BOOK OF LAWS, is for "WE THE PEOPLE." It takes care of the fundamental things we need, such as freedom, security, and protection from bondage, and provides the opportunity for success through understanding its truths. (Joshua 1:8)

The Bible and the Constitution work like an American or European football game. There must be laws (rules) and referees; the Holy Spirit is the referee for the believer. He ensures that all the players conduct themselves within the game's laws. Typically, the team performing more carefully within the laws (rules) is victorious. Although for the believer, the Lord guarantees victory now and in the future. This book does not put us in bondage. Instead, it leads us to freedom! Job and his friends dialogued for thirty-seven chapters. They were attempting to discover the truth of the *why* Job had experienced sickness and tragedy in epic proportions.

A change of focus from WHY to HOW?

In chapter thirty-eight, God finally speaks to Job, but he does not answer the questions about Job's guilt or innocence or *why* he has experienced such sickness and tragedy. Instead, God speaks about the created order of the universe and reveals His omnipotence to Job.

Throughout the first thirty-seven chapters of the book, Job and his friends were darkening wise counsel by haphazardly speaking words without knowledge. (Job 38:2) Interestingly enough, before God starts to unload a myriad of questions on Job, He orders Job to "gird" himself. (Job 38:3 KJV, Job 40:7 KJV) God gave Job a direct order to surround himself with true and accurate knowledge.

Throughout the last five chapters of the book of Job, God explained to Job *how* to overcome. The Bible has more "how to overcome answers" and less dialogue on why things happen. I recovered from childhood trauma by seeking my *how* to overcome it. Like Job, I made a personal application for restoration and victory:

1. Job spoke negatively about things he did not understand to appear righteous and justified. (Job 40:8) Never condemning God became my priority, even if I didn't understand or know what He was doing in my life.

2. How did Job respond to this newfound knowledge? He repented. *"I take back everything I said and sit in dust and ashes to show my repentance."* (Job 42:6 NLT) Repentance to the Lord is a prerequisite for healing, wholeness, and restoration. Jesus told His disciples that they had the power to speak to a situation, and if they did not doubt, it would be done. (Mark 11:23) He continued, and when you stand praying about your situation, Jesus said to forgive if you have something against anyone, so your prayers will not be hindered. (Mark 11:25 KJV). Yes, it's imperative that you understand that any unforgiveness will hinder your prayers from being answered.

3. Job prayed and forgave his friends, although not an easy task. (Job 42:9 NKJV). One of his friends suggested that Job's training of his children could be to blame (Job 8:4) Job had seven sons and three daughters, and in one day, he lost all of them. It had only been a few days since Job and his wife had lost their ten children, and Job's friend Eliphaz started with his criticism. Eliphaz makes the case that if the father sins and suffers, so will his offspring.

> He said, *"I have seen the foolish taking root [and outwardly prospering], but suddenly I saw that his dwelling was cursed [for his doom was certain]. His children are far from safety; [involved in their father's ruin] they are crushed in the [court of justice in the city's] gate, and there is no one to deliver them."* (Job 5:3-4 AMPC)

Can you imagine your closest friends coming to you in your time of bereavement, and you're expecting comforting words, only to receive criticism that makes things worse?

I often think that if Job can forgive his friends, we should be able to forgive anyone.

Regardless of what was said or the horrific actions of others, like Job, your commission is to forgive. The law of forgiveness clearly states that if we refuse to forgive anyone, our heavenly father will not forgive us. (Mark 11:26)

After Job had met these three conditions, the Lord restored his fortunes. (Job 42:10) Job experienced the supernatural hand of God by girding himself with the truth. When the believer is obedient to work carefully within the laws (book), particularly the laws of faith, miracles and the supernatural happens. (Romans 3:27) I believe it is impossible to work within the Laws of Faith, surrounding us with truth, and not experience a miracle or the supernatural.

Chapter Fifteen

FAITH DOES NOT SIT AND COMPLAIN, FAITH GOES AND DOES

MANY YEARS AGO, Tarsha and I purchased a large historic home for our rescue mission ministry. Although the house was built in 1929, it had some good bones. The only major issue was the outdated septic system. It was no surprise that the septic system needed updating; the surprise came while standing in the home's basement with the plumber. He noted the basement has eight-and-a-half foot ceilings, so the septic tank is at least nine feet underground somewhere in the half-acre field. The former owner was deceased, and we did not know its location.

The plumber explained that he would typically use a soil probe to find systems four feet or less below the surface, but my system's exact location would require heavy digging equipment to resolve the problem. Mr. Plumber had a theory; he would trace the lines from the basement to the field and find its location. The following day he arrived with big trucks and heavy equipment. The plumber's boss immediately jumped out of the truck and asked the location of the tank. I explained that the place was unknown. Mr. Bossman, a.k.a. "Mr. Attitude," could not believe I would have him bring his equipment, not knowing the location. I waited patiently for Mr. Plumber to speak up and tell Mr. Attitude; that this was his idea and get me out from "under the bus."

He never said a word about it but told the boss that he had a theory and marked a few places based on the plumbing running from the basement. He took three shovels and stuck them in the ground in various areas the digging should occur. Mr. Attitude told me his meter had started, and they could work all day and not find anything. He exclaimed that finding a four-by-four-foot-long top to the septic tank in a half-acre field is like trying to find a needle in a haystack. Furthermore, he added, "This day is going to be expensive for you!"

Get your rump off the complaining stump

His spoken words became a belt of truth for a moment as they unsuccessfully dug the first hole. I found a stump and sat on it with head in hands, repeating to the Lord what Mr. Attitude had said. "Lord, this will be an expensive day for me!" "This is like finding a needle in a haystack!" I patiently waited for a response from the Lord, and He said absolutely nothing. So, I went a little further and with more passion. "Lord, this house is for your Kingdom's work; how can this situation happen to us?" "I deserve an answer!" I waited for any response, and the Lord did not answer.

At that moment, I thought, "Michael, you are in the middle of a test; the teacher is quiet while the student is testing." I said, "Oh boy, this is exam day."

Look for a behavior change

I thought, "Michael if you do not change your behavior, you have not learned anything." An accurate self-examination of whether you have grown in an area is to check your behavior the next time you have a crisis. I asked myself, what have you learned about this book of the law and putting on the belt of truth? A familiar scripture came to mind. "The Lord God is a Sun and Shield; He gives grace and glory, no good thing will He withhold from them, that walk uprightly." (Psalm 84:11)

Immediately, I arose from my stump of complaining and began to confess. "No good thing will he withhold from me!" "Finding the location of this tank is a good thing, and You are not refusing to give me good things!

Hallelujah!" Faith does not sit and complain! Faith goes and does! The Holy Spirit said, "Get a shovel and walk the field." I pulled one of the shovels out of the ground and began to walk the field. Mr. Attitude was on the back of the tractor digging while two of his staff were standing on the ground. They watched as I walked the area with that shovel tightly gripped.

They enjoyed an excellent momentary laugh. However, I was not bothered; it made me more determined. His truth of Psalm 84:11 had surrounded me like a belt! If I was concerned about my reputation, I knew that I would not experience a miracle. Jesus made himself of no reputation (Philippians 2:7), and I had to imitate Him regardless of what anyone thought or said.

Moreover, the shovel got heavy at a particular place in the field; The Holy Spirit said, "Put it in this spot." The teacher had spoken. It was as if the professor was saying, "Testing time is up! Put your pens and pencils down!" I immediately did so and told Mr. Attitude to dig in that particular spot. Elevating his voice over the machine's noise, he sarcastically laughed and said, "Okay, buddy, you are the boss. Whatever you say!"

He dug about four to five feet down, and his two staff jumped in the hole using the soil probes to see if anything was there. They said this hole is like the three others; there is nothing here but dig down another few feet to ensure. He dug another few feet and scraped the center of that four-by-four septic tank top. The three men were in total disbelief at what had just happened.

They were lost for words as they nervously looked at one another. A short time later, when Mr. Attitude had time to process and pull himself together, he turned off his equipment and asked, "how did you do that?"

I said to him, "It could have been luck." He said he has been in the business for more than thirty years, and there is no way this could have been luck. He said he had never seen anything like it or even heard of something like this happening before. So, I told him the Holy Spirit that lives inside of me, and inside, every believer instructed me where to put the shovel.

He said he is not a church-going man, but he knew it had to be something. I discussed with him that a relationship with Christ is good for finding septic tank tops, but He will also help His followers navigate all their life issues.

I invited him to receive Christ and become a follower; he said he would seriously consider it but rejected the invitation at that moment. Ironically, as I was walking away, he yelled across the field and offered me a job with an excellent salary and benefits. I quickly yelled back, "The Holy Spirit doesn't work like that, and I would not be any good to your company!" Even unbelievers are attracted when signs and wonders accompany the believers.

If you are in a season that seems like the Holy Spirit is silent, perhaps you have found yourself in the middle of your exam. Interestingly, you will determine the length of your exam. If I had not changed my behavior (attitude), my "exam" day could have been extended and expensive.

In the Book of Deuteronomy, Moses explained to the Israel community how rebellion caused an eleven-day journey (exam) to take forty years to complete. (Deuteronomy 1:2-3) The instructions were to go and occupy the land the Lord had promised. (Deuteronomy 1:21) Nevertheless, the community rebelled and refused to go in. (Deuteronomy 1:26) Afterward, the Lord commanded them to go back through the wilderness toward the Red Sea, and once again, they rebelled. Their failure to comply caused the Holy Spirit to go silent in their lives.

> [45] *Then you returned and wept before the Lord, but the Lord did not listen to your voice, nor pay attention to you.* [46] *So you remained at Kadesh for many days, the days that you spent there.* (Deuteronomy 1:45-46 NASB)

It was not until they followed their last instructions before He spoke again. Parents are often frustrated when their children repeatedly ask about the previously given instructions. Perhaps the children continue to ask because they disagree with the last instructions and hope that the instructions will change.

As it was with the children of Israel, they remained in the same area for an extended time, hoping God would change His mind. They were conducting themselves like children; perhaps that is why the scriptures refer to them as the Children of Israel more than five hundred times. Nevertheless, they eventually made an adult decision, turned around, and headed back into the wilderness, and the Holy Spirit spoke to them again.

> [1] *"Then we turned around and headed back across the wilderness toward the Red Sea, just as the Lord had instructed me, and we wandered around in the region of Mount Seir for a long time.* [2] *"Then, at last, the Lord said to me,* [3] *'You have been wandering around in this hill country long enough; turn to the north.* (Deuteronomy 2:1-3 NLT)

The exam was complete. It proves that the Holy Spirit is a great teacher and will not pass us to the next level simply because we have been in Holy Spirit Class 101 for forty years, but the Lord's invisible shields will expedite the process.

The heart guard

In military battles, body armor is essential to a soldier's equipment. According to roman military.net, the Roman army in 160 BC wore body armor with only a twenty-centimeter square breastplate, called a heart guard. The military believed that armor was essential to a soldier's equipment. Although the technology of the soldier's armor has changed, the purpose is still the same; to protect and preserve life. The design of the Roman soldier's heart guard protected against spears, javelins, arrows, and swords. Out of all the organs of our bodies, the Bible has deemed the heart the most important. King Solomon was undoubtedly one of the wisest men that ever lived. In Proverbs Chapter 4, he said,

> *"20 My son, give attention to my words; Incline your ear to my sayings. 21 Do not let them depart from your eyes; Keep them in the midst of your heart; 22 For they are life to those who find them, and health to all their flesh. 23 Keep your heart with all diligence, for out of it spring the* <u>issues</u> *of life.»* (Proverbs 4:20-23 NKJV)

According to Merriam-Webster, "issue" is a condition or occurrence traceable to a cause. Solomon makes a direct connection to how our spoken words affect our health. Solomon's appeal is for you to guard your heart above all else constantly. *The Amplified Bible (Classic Edition)* refers to this armor as the breastplate of integrity, moral rectitude, and right standing with God (Ephesians 6:14). The believer's integrity operates as a heart guard.

In our hearts is where we understand that Grace happens when the righteousness of Christ is imputed to us. It means we are declared "not guilty" because of all Christ did for us on the cross—we experience a change of status. The righteousness of Christ is imparted to us—it becomes a part of us, and we undergo a change of heart. Day by day, we become more like Christ in our attitudes and actions. (Ephesians 3:14-19. Having been born again and justified through grace (the just-if-I'd never sinned grace), we will grow and mature spiritually.

A friend had his health physical followed by a conversation with his primary care physician. As they discussed one portion of the test that he assumed would have better results, he explained that the issue was in his DNA and passed down. Our family name and specific characteristics were imputed and handed down to us. As we mature in the word, we grow into those characteristics that the Holy Spirit has imparted to us, and they become our own, perfecting us in the image of God and the likeness of Jesus Christ. It is a lifelong process of dying to what is evil and rising to what is good with the help of the Spirit of Christ.

> *So, the gifts of the Spirit help us grow and build up the body of Christ.* (1 Corinthians 12-14)

As we mature as Christians, our lives display certain qualities known as the fruit of the Spirit.

> *"The fruit of the Spirit is love, joy, peace, patience, kindness, generosity, faithfulness, gentleness, and self-control."* (Galatians 5:22 NKJV)

As you know, maturing involves perfecting and pruning. (John 15:2 NKJV) The Bible tells us that God prunes the branches that bear fruit so they will produce even more, and every vine and fruit tree requires pruning, and so do we. Life is a journey, and at times the journey is painful.

However, God says, " Such hope never disappoints or deludes or shames us, for God's love has been poured into our hearts through the Holy Spirit that has been given to us." (Romans 5:5 AMPC) You do not deserve or earn the love of God; you open your heart to receive it.

Live to make a difference and not to make a living, and the living will take care of itself

Some stories stick with me, whether actual or false; they seem to engrave themselves in my memory bank. Like the first time I listened to the story of Nehemiah. His non-fictional tale is one of the greatest of the Old Testament but perhaps not discussed as much as others. Nehemiah's heart was burdened with rebuilding Jerusalem's walls, thus rebuilding Jerusalem's city.

In ancient cities, walls symbolized security, strength, protection, and the only natural means of defense. Some walls were as much as twenty-five feet thick and over three hundred feet in height. Those walls were massive! Nehemiah's wall was considered very important; it took six chapters to cover the reconstruction of the walls around Jerusalem. (Nehemiah 1–7:73 NKJV)

I find it very interesting that six chapters covered the reconstruction of the walls, so much so that I sense that on occasions, we need to rebuild walls in our personal lives. Sometimes, it requires a total reconstruction. Moreover, other times, perhaps a little "patchwork" will do.

If we work His words into our lives, we will be like a competent carpenter who dug deep and laid the foundation of his house on a bed of rocks. When the river burst its banks and crashed against the house, nothing could shake it; He built it to last.

Nevertheless, if we use His words in Bible studies and general conversations and never work them into our personal lives, we will be like the witless carpenter who built his house but skipped the foundation phase. When the swollen river came crashing in, it collapsed like a house of cards. It was a total loss. (Matthew 7 MSG Bible) Rebuilding walls in our lives is like re-establishing security, strength, protection, and purpose.

In my personal life of living to make a difference, I have the honor of encountering human derelicts, drifting up and down the streets with an absolute sense of hopelessness and helplessness. Furthermore, I often share that life transformation begins when a person first becomes greatly concerned about their ruins. When Nehemiah paused long enough to assess the walls, he sat down, wept, and mourned for days.

Life transformation follows a time of reassessing the ruins, like Nehemiah, perhaps going through a season of weeping and mourning and then developing a plan to rebuild. When we live to make a difference and not make a living, the living will care for itself. And we will soon discover that no wall is beyond repair.

>*"Where success is concerned, people are not measured in inches, or pounds, or college degrees, or family background; they are measured by the size of their thinking."* (David J Schwartz (2016). "The Magic of Thinking Big," p.84)

So then, as Harriet Tubman said, "If you hear the dogs, keep going; if you see the torches in the woods, keep going. Suppose there is shouting, after you, keep going. Do not ever stop. Keep going. If you want a taste of freedom, keep going." Blackalliance.org

It is possible for you to live your dreams and impact the world if you simply keep going!

Printed in the USA
CPSIA information can be obtained
at www.ICGtesting.com
LVHW010851290923
759457LV00018B/781

9 781662 873898